The Craft
of
Black Work
and
White Work

ERICA WILSON

CHARLES SCRIBNER'S SONS / NEW YORK

1 3 5 7 9 11 13 15 17 19 M/P 20 18 16 14 12 10 8 6 4 2

Printed in the United States of America
Library of Congress Catalog Card Number 75-27383
ISBN 0-684-14496-4

CONTENTS

Snail, showing stitches in large scale on coarse white linen. Grass in chain stitch using gold lurex. *Designed and worked by author*

BLACK WORK

ITEM: *One paire of shetys of fyne Hollande clothe, wroughte with Spanysshe worke of blacke silke upon the edgies.*

—FROM AN INVENTORY OF THE WARDROBE OF CATHERINE OF ARAGON

By the Lady Jebson, one smock all over wrought with black silk, the sleeves wrought with gold.

—QUEEN ELIZABETH'S NEW YEAR GIFT, 1561

BLACK work, a form of embroidery which uses black silk and gold thread on cream linen, originated in Spain, and rose to the zenith of its popularity in sixteenth-century England.

Compared with the magnificent exuberance of other Elizabethan embroideries, black work has a delicacy and restraint which, above all other work of that time, shows a tremendous strength and style. Beautifully formalized flowers, enclosed by sweeping stems and strong outlines, were worked with lacy filling stitches by counting the threads of the fine white linen background. The whole design was often enriched by the sparkle of gold thread and a powdering of "owes" (better known today as sequins) to make it glisten.

So many influences and types of embroidery probably contributed to its origin that it is very difficult to say exactly where and when black work began. By the 1400's Spain had been under the domination of the Moors for eight centuries, and the interlaced strapwork patterns and geometric designs which were characteristic of Spain at this time were the ones which appeared first in England, being used generally for borders, done with great lightness and delicacy in a stitch called double running.

Looking at the geometric, bold contrasts of Arab designs, sometimes woven and re-embroidered, which have changed so little through the centuries, it is easy to see where the roots of black work began. Then, through its growth in Spain, and its final blossoming in England as a style all its own, we can see how other influences, such as the beginnings of printing and the popularity of wrought-iron work and even the ubiquitous Celtic strapwork coming down through the centuries, all played their part in forming its final beauty.

Black work—or Spanish work as it was often called—had undoubtedly been done in England before the 1500's. Chaucer refers to it in his *Canterbury Tales.*

> Whit was hir smok, and broyden al bifoore,
> And eke bihynde, on hir coler aboute,
> Of colblak silk withinne and eke withoute,
> The tapes of hir white voluper
> Were of the same suyte of hir coler.

OPPOSITE. Panel for a man's vest—black silk, cotton, and gold thread on white linen. *Designed and worked by author*

And in 1493 John Wylgryse of Coventry left among his effects a *"Pintheamen consutum cum serico nigro."*

Around the time of the arrival of Catherine of Aragon in England in 1501, black work began to be more popular than ever before. Fortunately, we have whole galleries of oil paintings to show us in exact detail what the black embroidery on ruff and cuff, on partelett and bodice, on sleeve and jacket, was like; the portrait painters paid as much attention to the magnificent costume as to the sitters themselves. Perhaps with reason, for the artist who painted the portrait might well have been also attached to the household to design embroideries for costume and furnishings.

At first, the embroidery was mainly done on fine linen for the neck ruffs and frilled cuffs of shirts. When outer sleeves were slashed to allow the shirt to show through, then the sleeve underneath had to be decorated, and eventually the top sleeve was in two pieces, just caught together in several places at the edges. As time progressed, patterns became more elaborate and black silk embroidery was used all over the sleeves, stom-

Black work sampler, English, 16th century. *Victoria and Albert Museum*

achers, bodices and caps, on gloves, on handkerchiefs, and on hoods. The stomacher, or partelett, mentioned above, was a long inverted triangle which filled in the bodice. Very often it had sleeves—which were detach-able—embroidered to match it. One of Queen Elizabeth's New Year gifts in 1601 was "A partelett and a peire of sleeves of sypress wrought with silver and black silke."

But black work was not restricted only to costume. The Elizabethans loved to make themselves comfortable. Beds were hung with silk and embroideries, and sometimes had as many as three different coverlets made to match the hangings. The reason for this is explained when one reads the Hardwick Hall inventory for My Lady's Bed Chamber: "A coverlett to hang before a dore . . . three coverlets to hang before a windowe . . . a counterpoynt (coverlet) of tapestrie before an other dore. . . ."

All this finery would be on view, for the bedroom was not then the private place it is today. Carved oak benches and chairs would have soft cushions specially made to fit them; but the "pillow-beres" which were so popular for black-and-gold embroidery would probably have been used on the bed itself, designed to be framed by being surrounded with plain white "Holland" linen, or a simple quilted coverlet. Being more flexible and softer than needlework on canvas or embroidery in silk and metal threads, black work was particularly suitable for use in the bedroom, even for night shirts, which were just beginning to be worn. Up until this time, people either went to bed naked, or slept in the shirts or smocks they had worn underneath during the day. The whole idea of special bedclothes was new. Nightcaps, sometimes enriched with that most difficult stitch, the plaited braid stitch, in gold thread, would be worked in fine designs of tiny black stitches.

> and the beau would feign sickness to
> show his nightcap fine

. . . . and before retiring he would rub his teeth with a linen cloth edged with silver lace instead of a toothbrush! "From Mistress Twist, the Court laundress; Four tooth cloths of holland, wrought with black work and edged with bone lace of silver and black silk. . . ."

Later, the nightcap became so beautiful it was not worn in bed for sleeping but in the house during the day. Sir Walter Raleigh even wore one to the scaffold, under his hat, and gave it to a bystander who was cold. The latter may not have been a customary fashion, though, for it was a bitter cold day when Sir Walter Raleigh was executed and he was afraid that he might shiver and that this would be mistakenly interpreted as fear.

The nightcap was really the man's equivalent of the woman's coif, which was so often edged with lace made of silver or gold thread, and like the coif was decorated closely with beautiful patterns in fine stitchery. The overall lines of stem tracery enclosed the motifs inside them. Peas, whose golden pods could be lifted up to disclose the seed pearl peas within; strawberries, the most decorative and popular of all fruits, costing one penny a bushel at the time; grapes; flowers of every kind; beasts and butterflies—all were stitched with black and gold threads on the fine white linen. Some designs were obviously inspired by engravings and woodcuts, and were worked entirely with a speckling stitch which imitated this, called seeding (right, below), instead of the counted diaper patterns which gave the effect of beautiful appliquéd lace.

A nightcap. *Montreal Museum of Fine Arts*

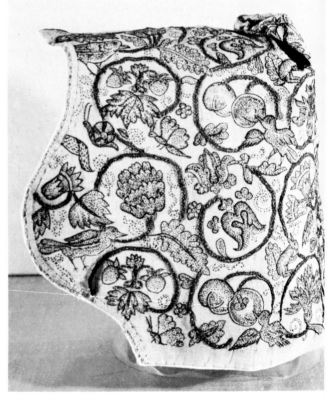

A cap with speckling. *Cooper Hewitt Museum of Design, Smithsonian Institution*

Portrait of Mary Cornwallis by George Gower, showing sleeves with black work embroidery under fine lawn. *City Art Gallery, Manchester*

Sometimes black work would be covered or veiled with a soft transparent lawn, perhaps to protect it, perhaps to soften the sharp black-and-white contrasts to better suit the less brilliant climate of England than its country of origin, Spain, or simply perhaps because new linens enabled a very fine thread to be spun, and the novelty of a transparent cloth would be too fascinating to be ignored. We read of "his wrought pillow overspread with lawn," and, from Ben Jonson, "Shadow their glorie as the Milliner's wife doth her wrought stomacher with a smoakie lawne or a blacke cipress."

Linen cambric became so fine it was called cobweb lawn, and Henry VIII, while playing tennis, was much admired for a shirt of such transparent linen gauze that his "blond skin shone through."

Old inventories always list "Spanysh work" separately from "Black work," but without being able to see the actual embroidery they describe it is impossible to tell whether the names were really interchangeable. It seems probable, however, that Spanish work was used to describe the

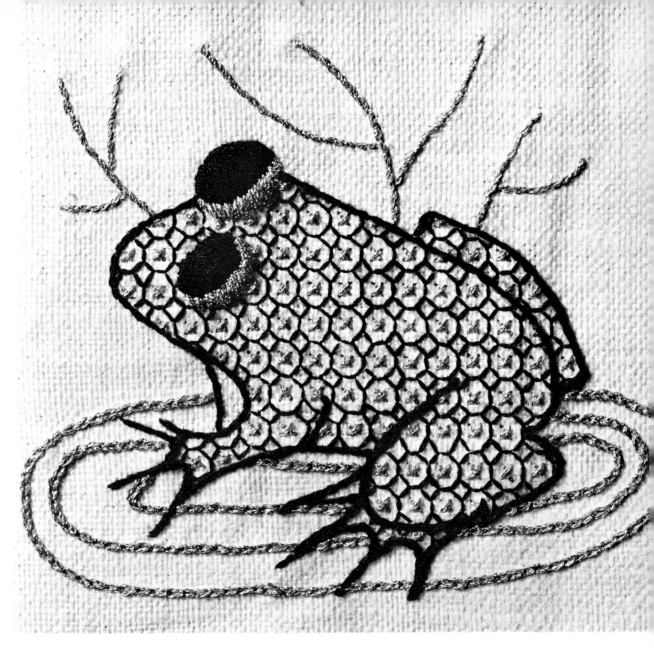

Large stitches used for bold effect. *Designed and worked by the author*

earlier double running and darning patterns that were more familiar in Spain, and that black work came to be synonymous with the later black-and-gold embroidery done with filling stitches or seeding. Often the double running was known as Holbein stitch, because Holbein's portraits so often showed designs of this kind. Sometimes, though more rarely, they were worked in red instead of black, and were seen throughout the Continent as well as in England.

OPPOSITE. Modern use of Holbein stitch or reversible double running on table linen. *Author's collection*

Four hundred years later we still have a remarkable number of exquisite black work embroideries in our museums. Unfortunately, the silk has badly worn in some of them, but when you consider a typical recipe for the black dye you wonder how they have lasted at all!

> 15 lb Elderbark
> 12 lb of soot (oak shavings or sawdust)
> 10 lb vitriol
> 2 lb wild marjoram
> 6 lb brown wood
> $1\frac{1}{2}$ lb Calcined Allom and Vitriol mixed
> 4 lb Filings
> as much lye as necessary
> 10 lb Walnut shells.

Black work was popular throughout the sixteenth century, perhaps because Mary Tudor's consort Philip II still maintained England's link with its country of origin, but since then little black work has been done.

To collect a sampler nowadays of the many beautiful black work fillings is an idea which could lead to all sorts of combinations. The size and scale of present-day black work can be varied according to temperament, but enlargement in stitches in itself gives the embroidery a fascinatingly contemporary appearance. The following pages may inspire some idea of what is possible, not forgetting that "black and gold" may also be effectively combined with other types of embroidery.

TO BEGIN

Black work must be done on an evenly woven material, because part of its effect is working geometric stitches to fill the different areas of design, using a monochromatic color scheme. It really looks beautiful when worked with fine black silk on a crisp white linen with gold thread, but it can also be embroidered with blue and silver, or red and white, or green and gold. On page 56 is a design worked with white thread on black linen to give a reversed effect.

Black work lends itself, among other things, to evening bags, picture panels, mirror frames, boxes, table linen, vests, and cushions. Traditionally its nature is fine, delicate, and sophisticated, but it would be interesting to experiment with bolder effects—perhaps even working a carpet on needlepoint canvas with coarse rug wool, making the lacy repeat patterns very large in black wool, and filling the background in with white tent stitch.

It is a good idea to begin by collecting some of the black work stitches on linen so that you can see their effect. They look so entirely different when they are worked, compared with their effect in a photograph or drawing. Only when it is embroidered can you see how the same pattern done in bold crewel wools can look utterly changed from one done in fine black silk. Then you can use this sampler to refer to when you are embroidering your main design.

Companion picture to the frog, page 12
Designed and worked by the author

CHOOSING FABRICS

Fine, evenly woven white linen is the traditional fabric, but monk's cloth or coarse white linen, even nylon or coarse wool material, would be excellent for black work as long as the weave is regular enough. There is an oriental wallpaper which is manufactured with widely spaced canvas—a white linen weave thread laminated to a white paper background. These threads are spaced out evenly and held in place by the paper backing, making this firm fabric most suitable for pictures and panels in bold black work. Alternatively, you could use a regular needlepoint canvas with single weave (mono), leaving the canvas open as a background and backing it afterward with white fabric.

The most important thing is to find a material with a clear even weave, as all the stitch patterns have to be counted out on the background following the mesh.

Match the thickness of your working thread to your background material. Your working threads should be approximately the same thickness as those in the fabric.

TOP, LEFT TO RIGHT. Black linen; even weave canvas wall covering; the same in natural
BOTTOM, LEFT TO RIGHT. White coarse-weave linen; medium-weave linen; monkscloth, similar to "Binca" even weave cotton

THREADS AND NEEDLES

Fine fingering knitting wool or acrylic fiber, or fine tapestry wool are all good for black work, as they are rounded threads, smooth and not hairy—the better to work clear-cut, crisp, geometric patterns. Six-stranded mercerized cotton embroidery floss, buttonhole twist, or sewing silk are all good for finer effects. The best way is to collect various threads and try them out on your linen. As to the gold thread, various sewing companies put out a gold you can sew with—a fine Lurex variety which is nontarnishing. These may be sewn or couched onto the fabric and, together with sequins, are often the final touch—the frosting on the cake—which just finishes the design.

Use blunt (tapestry) needles in a size to correspond with the thickness of your wool and background fabric, so that you can pass between the threads of the linen without splitting them. For outlining, for gold threads, and for any patterns which are not worked by the thread of the linen, use sharp needles, either crewel or chenille, again large enough so that the threads pass easily through the linen. A specially large-eyed needle is necessary to protect the fragile gold thread as it passes back and forth through the fabric. When very fine, it is a good idea to knot the gold thread around the eye of the needle to prevent it from constantly slipping out.

BEGINNING THE DESIGN

Patterns for black work must necessarily be stylized, since the design is to be worked with geometric repeat fillings. This does not mean that your design must be limited to abstract shapes, or that the pattern must be made up of squares, circles, or triangles. It can consist of simple silhouette shapes, like those on the beautiful Elizabethan caps and bodices. These shapes may be filled with different lacy patterns worked both closely and lightly for contrast of texture—or blocks of the repeat patterns may make a design themselves, worked on a large scale (see pages 31-39).

Pictures in black work can be as strong and dynamic as a woodcut, or as delicate as the copies of early prints embroidered in speckling or seeding stitches (see page 45). A contemporary inspiration might be to work out a version of the much enlarged photos from newspapers or printed black-and-white photos, which, when blown up, appear as a series of large dots. The scissor-cut designs, or Scherenschnitte of Switzerland, with their beautiful silhouette shapes, are also excellent for black work (see page 18).

Before you begin to embroider, make a "cartoon" or drawing of your final design on paper, and fill in the areas to be stitched with three shades of any color: light, medium, and dark. You can do this with pencil, paint, or felt pens. This will show you which areas should be worked with close solid stitching (painted dark) which should be medium, and

A contemporary example of decorative black work showing the importance of contrasting solid black areas with light, open stitch patterns. Note the difference in effect on the upper flower where the same pattern is worked using a single thread of cotton in bold scale and with two threads of cotton in finer scale. *Designed and worked by Mrs. Grover O'Neill*

Swiss Scherenschnitte or silhouette work

which light and airy (painted light). *The effectiveness of the whole thing relies on your good balance between solid and open stitching.* Therefore, it is best to see this finished effect on your cartoon first, since any unpicking is apt to leave the material looking tired and gray!

Once you have applied your pattern by the methods on pages 19–23 (deciding which one seems most suitable for your background fabric), you will be ready to begin the stitching. You will find it much easier to count the threads of the linen if it is stretched tight in an embroidery frame or hoop (see page 24). If you are using gold thread, work with a square or stretcher frame since round hoops might squash and split the metallic threads.

Stylized designs to use for black work

APPLYING THE DESIGN

Whether you draw your own design or whether you adapt a pattern, it really takes no more skill to put your own design on fabric than it does to embroider the stitches. The following are some simple methods. You will be able to choose which method is best according to the texture of fabric you are working on. For smooth materials that are light in color the following is the quickest way of transferring the design.

APPLYING THE DESIGN WITH DRESSMAKERS' CARBON

Buy a packet of dressmakers' carbon from any notions department or sewing supply shop. (Ordinary carbon will smudge.) Fold the material in half and then in half again, and crease the folds so that they show clearly.

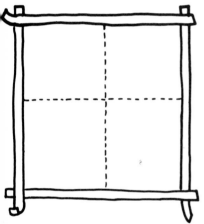

Then smooth the material flat on a table or board and hold it down evenly with masking tape on all four sides (as shown). A really smooth hard surface is necessary.

Fold the design, too, into four equal parts, open it up, and lay it down on top. Now slide a sheet of carbon paper, face downward, between paper and material. Use blue carbon for light materials, white for dark ones. Anchor the paper with some heavy weights (books, paperweights, etc.) and trace round the outline *very heavily* with a pencil. Using weights is a better idea than taping the design all round, because you can lift a corner occasionally to see how well the carbon is transferring. You really must *engrave* heavily to get good results, but you will soon find this out as you work.

Having folded the material, lay it out and fasten down with masking tape.

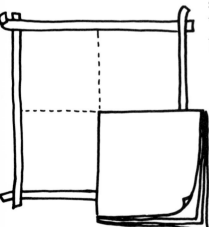

Fold the design into four parts and place it in position on one quarter of the fabric.

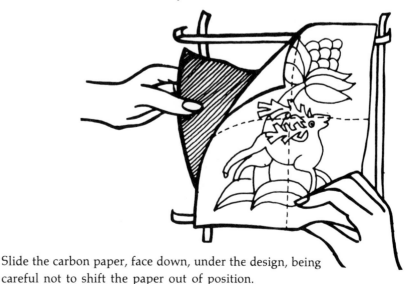

Slide the carbon paper, face down, under the design, being careful not to shift the paper out of position.

APPLYING THE DESIGN BY PERFORATION

(This method is best when design is to be used several times.)

1. Break a needle in half and set it into the eraser of an ordinary pencil. You will have to push the needle, blunt end first, into the eraser with a pair of pliers, then you will have a nice short pointed spike sticking out.

Set a needle into a pencil.

Prick the outlines of the design.

2. Trace the design onto a piece of layout or heavy tracing paper; lay this over a pad of felt, or any thick layer of material, placing a sheet of tissue between the two. Now prick holes with your spiked pencil all around the outlines, holding the pencil vertically—the holes should be fine and close, but as you practice your hand becomes like a machine, working fast and evenly.

3. First fold both fabric and perforation in four to find the center and hold it in place with weights (as in the carbon method). At a drugstore buy some *powdered* charcoal, and with a rolled and stitched pad of felt, or a blackboard eraser, rub the charcoal through the perforation you have made. Do this quite lightly, rubbing in a circular direction, without using too much charcoal. Lift a corner of the design to check, and if the line is not clear, rub through a little more "pounce" as the charcoal is called. If there is already too much, lift off the perforation and lightly blow off the surplus, leaving a clear line to follow with a brush.

Rub the charcoal through the pricking.

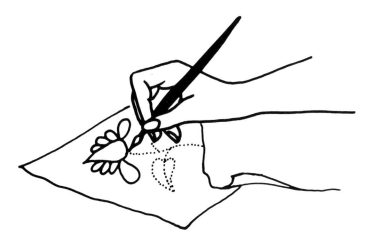

Paint around the outlines of the design.

4. Using a fine watercolor brush (#3 or #4) and a tube of blue watercolor paint, or gouache, paint around all the outlines. You will find the right mixture with practice—too much water, and the line will run, too much paint and it will not flow at all! Always begin at the edge nearest you, covering what you have done with a sheet of tissue paper, so that the pounce will not be smudged by your hand rubbing it. If you do not feel very much like an artist, use a fine, felt-tipped marker instead. Draw a line on the corner of the material first, to test the ink and see if it is fast. On dark material use white watercolor or gouache instead. Finally, bang the design hard with a clean cloth to remove the surplus charcoal. Rubbing will smudge it, so flick it until it is clean.

APPLYING THE DESIGN WITH A TRANSFER PENCIL

This product has arrived on the market lately and is a good short cut. Using the pink transferring pencil, outline the design on layout or tracing paper, then turn it face downward onto the material and iron like an ordinary commercial transfer, using a fairly warm iron. The one disadvantage is that it is apt to rub off and it does not provide a very clear, fine line. It is therefore most useful for larger, bold designs.

Bold, even-weave wool, or textured linen or monk's cloth, may not take either paint or carbon well. In this case one satisfactory method is the one described next.

APPLYING THE DESIGN WITH NET

If your fabric is very "knubbly" and rough textured, and your design is bold in scale, use this method to transfer the pattern directly on the cloth. Trace the design onto regular net, using a rather heavy black permanent marker. Then pin the net in position on the cloth and trace it again, using the marking pen. The ink from the pen will pass through the holes of the net to the cloth, giving you a clear outline which is easy to follow. Adjust the thickness of your felt-tipped marking pen to the texture of the material.

Last but not least, perhaps you may want to let your stitches dictate your pattern, and not be regulated by any permanent lines on the cloth, yet need some guide lines to help you. In this case you can try the following method.

APPLYING THE DESIGN FREEHAND

Since you need only a rough suggestion of the pattern and not a detailed drawing, you have several choices. You can mark your design with blackboard or tailor's chalk, which will rub off whenever you want to remove it . . . and sometimes before, which is one of its disadvantages! To make more definite, clearer lines you could lightly mark the fabric with a watercolor felt-tipped pen, and then wash the fabric afterward if any unwanted lines are showing. (However, be sure first to test your fabric for washability.)

A "pillow-beere"
Victoria and Albert Museum

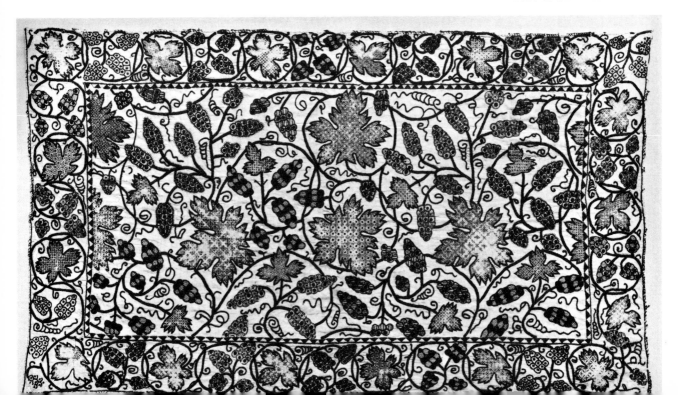

TRANSFERRING BLACK WORK PATTERNS TO FINE MATERIAL

To embroider cross stitch or any geometric design on fabric that does not have a clearly defined weave, baste a piece of single weave needlepoint canvas (mono) over the area where the pattern is to be. Stretch the whole thing in an embroidery frame and stitch the pattern through both thicknesses, keeping your stitches even by counting the threads of the canvas. When the design is finished, unravel the threads of the canvas at the edges and draw them right out, one by one. If your fabric is washable it may be easier to do this if you soak the embroidery in cold water. This softens the sizing in the canvas and loosens the threads enough to allow them to slip out easily.

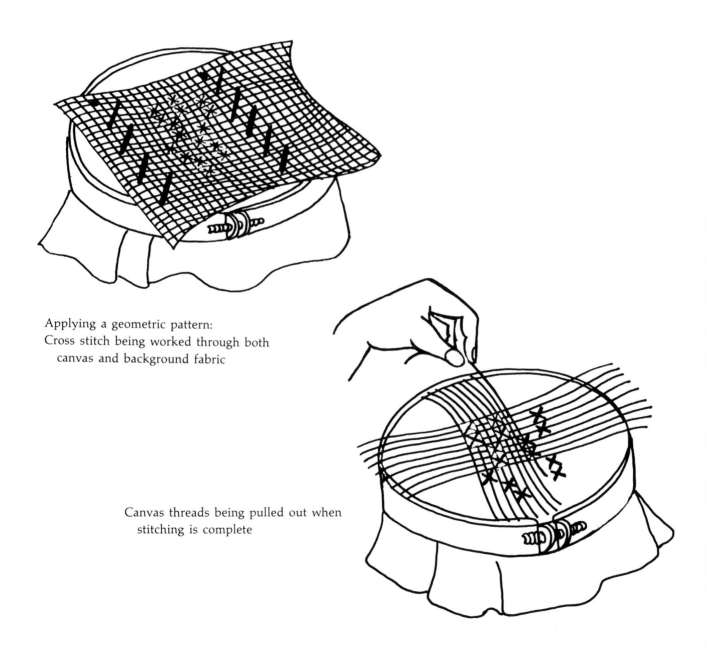

Applying a geometric pattern:
Cross stitch being worked through both
canvas and background fabric

Canvas threads being pulled out when
stitching is complete

CHOOSING A FRAME

First of all, is a frame really necessary? The answer is yes! The stitches of any embroidery—crewel, silk, and needlepoint—are easier to keep neat and even as long as the background fabric is stretched taut. Hoops and ring frames are the most versatile way to stretch out the fabric because you can work on articles of any size. (If your design is on too small a piece of material, simply stitch strips of linen or sheeting to the four sides to extend the fabric.) A floor stand goes one step further because it allows you to have both hands free for working, which greatly increases your speed and skill. In fact once you are accustomed to using this type of frame, you will never want to be without it.

The only disadvantage of a standing frame is that you can't carry it around with you very easily, so a more portable variety is a lap frame, which has been nicknamed the "fanny frame" because you can sit on it! This makes it very firm and yet flexible to work on—and means you can do your embroidery almost anywhere—in the car, the plane, at the meeting, at the hairdresser's, the office, even in bed!

Linen or wool fabrics and needlepoint canvas are tough and resilient, and therefore never get damaged by having the hoops pushed over them. Certain delicate materials or raised stitches, however, might be marked by a hoop, so place layers of tissue paper over the design before pushing the frame down. Then tear the paper away from the surface of the work, leaving it protecting the fabric round the edge where the hoop would be liable to chafe it. Alternatively, you have four other choices. One is to mount a piece of linen into the ring frame, and then baste your fabric to the linen on top of the frame, just where the design area is. Work through both layers, and then cut the linen away on the reverse side, all around the design area.

The second choice is to use a large oval rug or quilting hoop (see illustration) so that the material that is marked by the hoop will only be at the outer edges, which will not show. (The oval hoop is also useful for large-scale embroidery of any kind.)

The third choice is to work on a stretcher frame. Artists' stretcher frames, used for oil painting, come in all sizes and are available from almost every art store. You should buy a larger size than the finished measurement of your work to allow you to work right up to the edge of the design

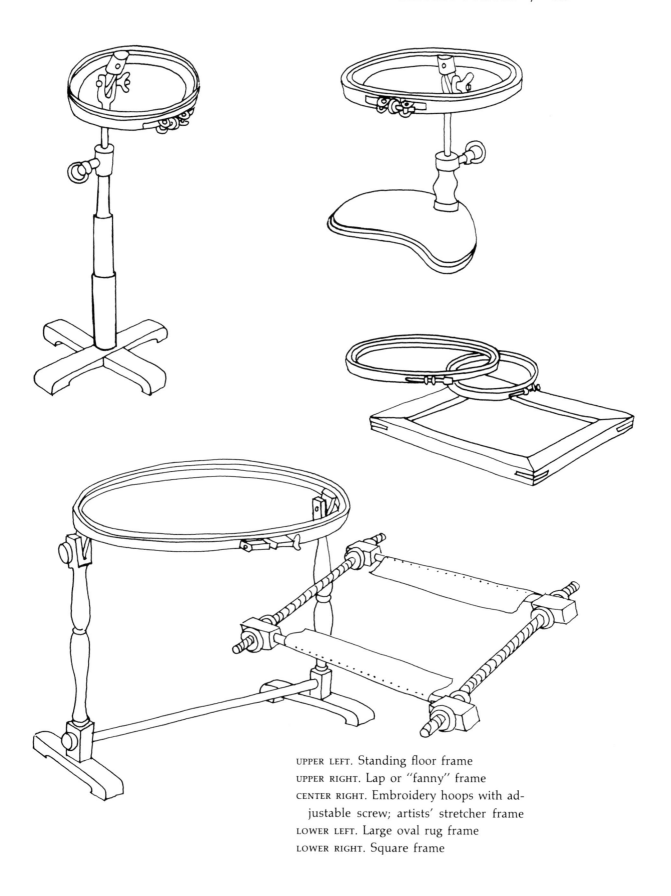

UPPER LEFT. Standing floor frame
UPPER RIGHT. Lap or "fanny" frame
CENTER RIGHT. Embroidery hoops with adjustable screw; artists' stretcher frame
LOWER LEFT. Large oval rug frame
LOWER RIGHT. Square frame

without the wooden strips getting in your way. Assemble the four strips and stretch your material tightly over the frame, thumbtacking or stapling the fabric to the back. Then work exactly as you would on an embroidery hoop. When finished, if the design is to be a panel, you have an "instant picture" ready to hang on the wall! If the material becomes slack while you are working on it, push some thread or material into the sides to make it tight.

The fourth choice is to use a square frame. This is delightful to work on since the material is always beautifully taut. The main disadvantage of a square frame is that it is awkward to move about. Secondly, it will only take material of the same width as itself. The length may be rolled around the rollers, but the width can only be that of the frame, 18 inches, 24 inches, or 36 inches (average frame sizes). So it is impossible to work a large bedspread on a square frame without having the frame made up to a special size. This is where a hoop frame, which is used just to stretch the area on which you are working, is especially useful.

It is perfectly possible, of course, to do embroidery in your hand. The only drawback is that certain stitches are eliminated from your repertoire. You cannot lay long threads across a surface, and tie them down afterward, for instance, unless you have a firm foundation to work on. A great many people do extremely neat work without using a frame at all, but for the average person a good effect is far more easily gained with its help. When using either a table or floor ring frame and both hands, the speed, dexterity, and ease with which you work will surprise you. *The stitches for which a frame is essential are marked with an asterisk on the stitch diagrams—all others can be worked without it.*

MOUNTING WORK IN A SQUARE FRAME

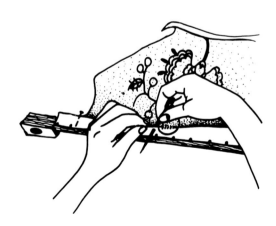

First stitch the fabric to the webbing of the square frame.

Then stretch tight, stitch webbing to either side and lace tightly with string as shown at right.

MOUNTING WORK IN A RING FRAME

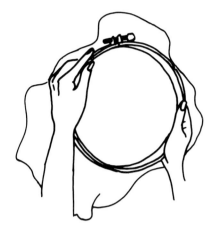

Before assembling the frame, adjust the screw so that the outer hoop fits snugly over the inner ring and the material. *Never* try to alter the screw when the frame is in place.

Pull the material taut; if the upper ring is tight enough the material will not slip back.

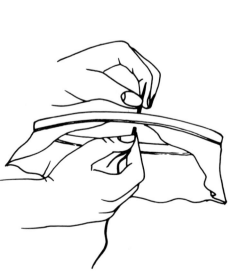

When the material is taut, push the upper ring down. To release the fabric do not unscrew the frame, but press thumbs down firmly into the fabric on the frame, at the same time lifting off the outer ring.

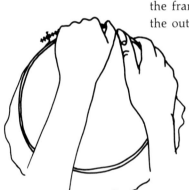

On any frame, always stab the needle up and down, never "sew." Work with both hands, keeping one *always* below the frame and the other above. This becomes much easier with practice and is essential for speed and dexterity.

STRETCHING AND BLOCKING

When an embroidery is finished it may be pressed or blocked. The latter is preferable, for pressing never brings out the very fine creases in heavy material like twill, and pressing is also inclined to pull the article out of shape. If, however, you wish to press an article such as a sweater which cannot be blocked, iron it on the wrong side into three or four thicknesses of toweling, using a damp cloth or steam iron. To block the finished work, first soak the embroidery in cold water, and lay it, dripping wet, on a board or old table which has been first covered with a sheet. If the embroidery is raised, lay it out right side uppermost; if it is flat and a smooth finished result is needed, put it right side down. Then, with carpet tacks, nail down the four corners first, measuring the opposite sides to see that they are even and making sure the corners are true right angles. You may have to pull the material out with pliers to make sure it is really taut. Then nail down four more tacks, one in the center of each side, and then eight more in the spaces between. Continue round and round, adding in this way more tacks until they are about $\frac{1}{4}$ inch apart. Allow the fabric to dry. When it is thoroughly dry, take it up, and if it is not being mounted immediately, roll it round a cardboard tube with the embroidery outward (so that the stitches are not crushed against one another).

When the black work design is finished, it can be blocked by the method described above. But if you have used gold threads which may tarnish, wetting the fabric may injure them. Therefore, press the design face downward into several layers of thick white Turkish toweling, using a damp cloth under the iron.

THE STITCHES

Whether you have begun by making a sampler, or whether you have launched right into your final design, practice the stitches you are going to use on the edge of your work, or on another piece of the same linen. Then you can see how they will work out on your particular cloth, and how they will look when you use *different thicknesses of thread* (see page 17). Try out both close and open stitches to see which are best in conjunction with one another.

The patterns are all counted onto the linen, but they are not complicated, for they are based on three simple stitches: cross, running, and back stitch. Always begin stitching in the center of each area to be filled, as it is much easier to count out one complete section of the pattern first than to start in an awkward corner where you will be interrupted by converging outlines. You can then fit the pattern into the corners, once you have established one or two unbroken repeats in the center. Combine the counted stitches with blocks of solid satin stitch for contrast, seeding, and all the squared fillings (see pages 42-45), using both black and gold threads for good variety. You can combine gold thread with the black silk or wool in other stitches, too; whipped stem and whipped chain are good for stems and outlines, using black thread and whipping in with gold, or vice versa (see pages 47, 49). Raised stem and raised buttonhole, braid stitch and raised spiders' webs are excellent stitched with plain gold threads. Sequins sewn down with matching yellow silk or a black French knot give richness to the design.

Below is a listing of the main and most important stitches used in black work. Those marked with an asterisk require using a frame.

BASIC BLACK WORK STITCHES	STITCHES FOR SOLID CONTRASTS AND OUTLINES	
Geometric counted stitches	Padded satin stitch	French knots
Darning stitches	Stem (plain and whipped)	Spiders' webs
Squared filling stitches	Chain (plain and whipped)	Braid stitch
Seeding	Raised stem, chain, and buttonhole	Bullion knots
		Buttonhole
		Laid work

Pillow with tree inspired by Scherenschnitte, backed with brilliant green velvet. *Designed and worked by the author*

*GEOMETRIC BLACK WORK STITCHES

Geometric Black Work stitches are counted out on to a regular weave background fabric and should always be worked with a blunt (tapestry) needle. Most black work patterns are based on two simple stitches, cross and back stitch. Try out the stitches as shown opposite and below. Then use the pages that follow as guides for other patterns. You will find that eventually you can make up your own.

*CROSS STITCH

Start with the easiest stitch which is Cross.

Using a blunt needle come up at A, count 3 threads up and 3 threads to the left, go down at B. Now count 6 threads to the right of B and come up at C.

Stitch CD repeats AB. Continue from E to F and G to H making a diagonal line of identical slanting stitches.

Now complete the cross by making stitches in the other direction from J to K so that you have a diagonal line of completed cross stitches. Each top stitch of the cross should always lie in the same direction for evenness. Once you have completed one diagonal line, make a pattern of diagonal lines which intersect on every other stitch as shown on the right of the diagram.

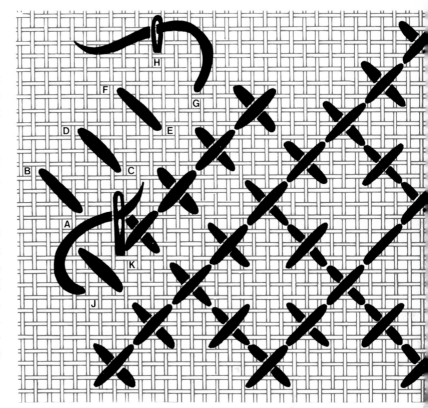

*BACK STITCH

Next try a pattern based on back stitch. Using a blunt needle, first practice back stitch as shown at right—up at A, down at B, up at C and down at A again. Then make the honeycomb pattern as shown on the left.

First make a series of slanting back stitches over 2 threads of the linen from A to B as shown.

Then work vertical stitches over 2 threads from C to D.

Complete the honeycomb with another line of stitches as in #1 and continue repeating steps 1, 2 and 3.

Finally, work a single vertical stitch over 2 threads in the center of each honeycomb.

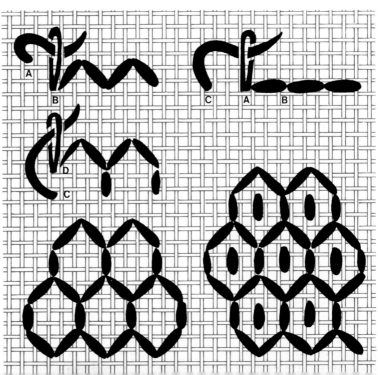

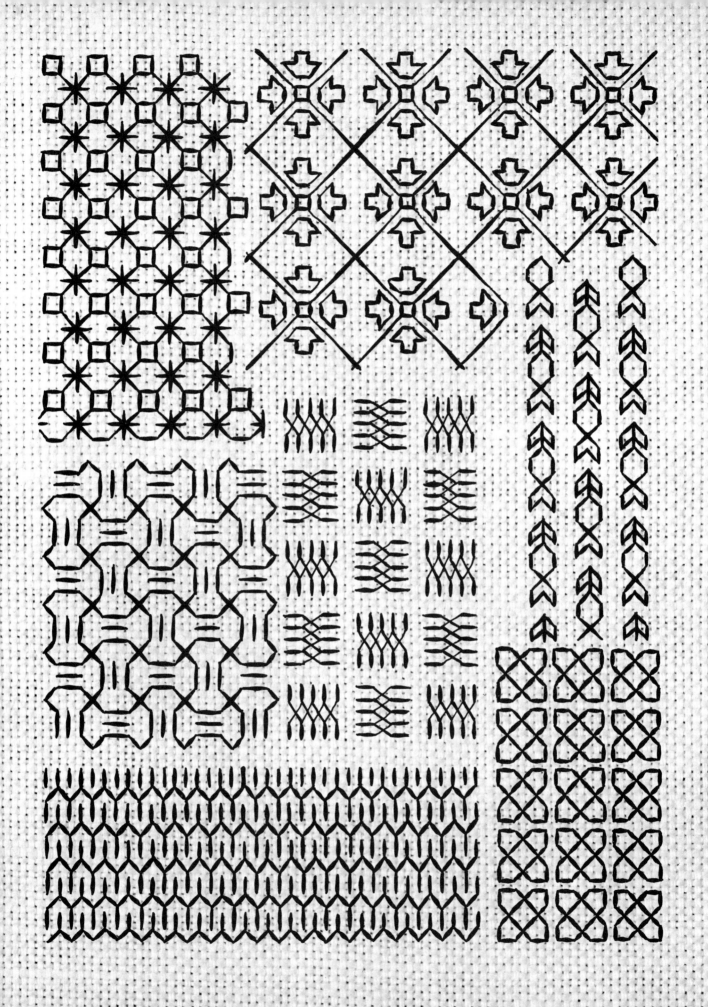

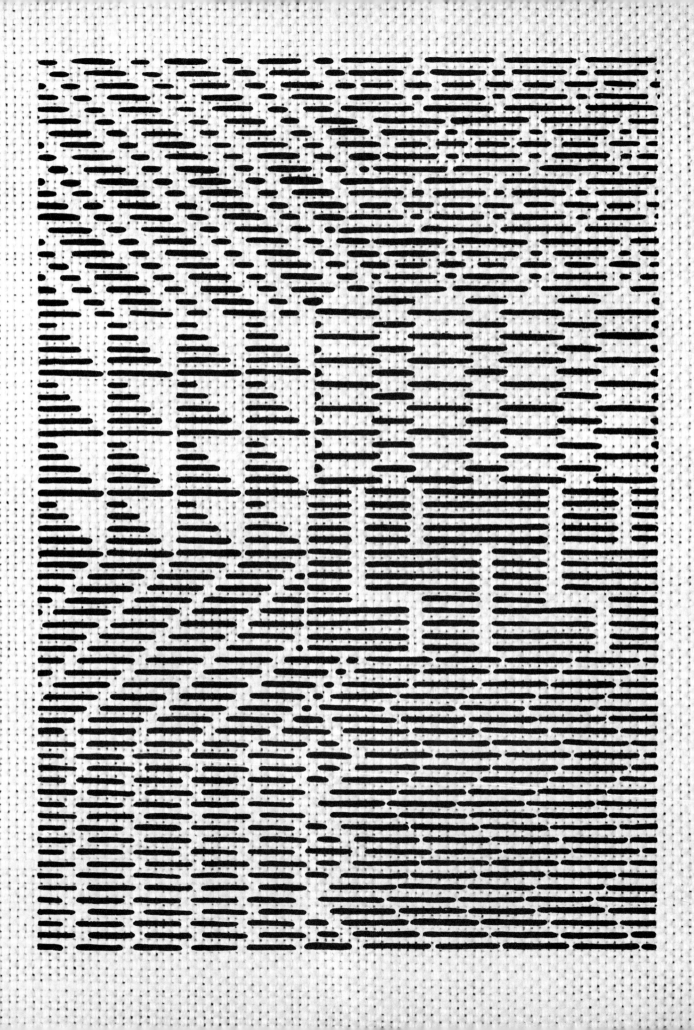

*DARNING STITCH

Using a blunt needle and a thread approximating the size of your linen, weave horizontal lines across the fabric to make the pattern shown below.

Come up at A, go over 7 threads, go down at B and under 3 threads.

Come up at C and go over 7 threads—again go down at D and continue, repeating these stitches along the line.

On the next line immediately below, come up 1 thread in from A and go over 5, under 2, over 1, under 2, and over 5 again. Repeat along the line.

On the next line come up 1 thread in from the line above and go over 3, under 2, over 3, and under 2.

Now repeat steps 4, 3, 2 and 1 in that order to form the diamond pattern as shown in the diagram. All kinds of patterns can be built up in this way as shown on the opposite page.

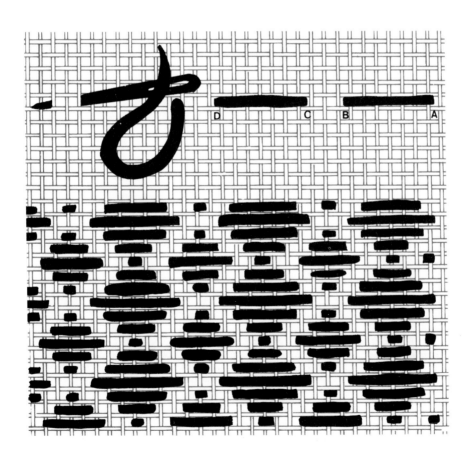

DOUBLE RUNNING

Using a blunt needle, come up at A, go over 3 threads and go down at B. Come up at C, 3 threads away and go down at D, over 3 more threads. Continue, making even stitches in a straight line.

Turn the work completely around and fill the spaces between with running stitches, going into the same holes as the previous ones to make a continuous line of stitching, alike on both sides.

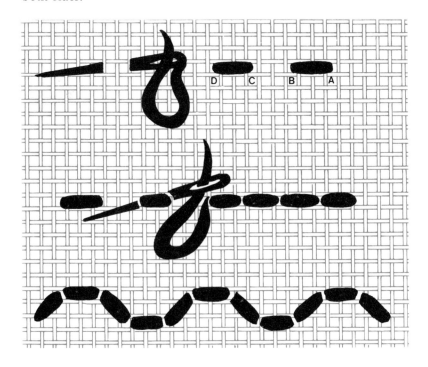

Double running or Holbein stitch. *Victoria and Albert Museum*

* SQUARED FILLING #1

The following are just a few of the many variations of Squared Fillings. Once you have grasped the basic idea, it is a simple matter to invent your own, and so add more to the collection. Squared Fillings are useful for breaking up plain areas, and it is possible to achieve unlimited color combinations with them. Squared Filling #3 may be shaded by changing the color in the blocks of Satin Stitch. All of them look best when used to fill stylized shapes and when combined with simple flat areas such as Laid Work in one color. They are so variegated in themselves that they need plain surroundings to set them off.

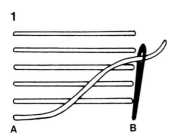

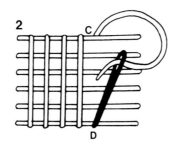

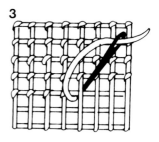

1. Coming up on one side of shape, make a long stitch right across, going down on other side. Fill the whole shape with exact parallel lines about ¼" apart.

2. Then lay threads in the opposite direction, making perfect squares.

4. Using a contrasting color, diagonally crisscross whole design with long lines, first in one direction across the center of every other square, then in the other direction so that the threads cross in the center of the basic squares.

5. With another contrasting color, tie down these diagonal lines where they cross in the center of the squares. This stitch should touch the basic squares at the top and bottom.

3. Tie down these squares at the corners with small stitches, all slanting in the same direction, as shown.

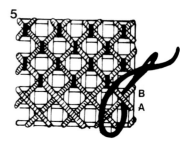

* SQUARED FILLING #2

Use a blunt (tapestry) needle for this stitch. Having laid long, parallel lines in one direction, go across in the other direction, but instead of laying the lines on top (as in squared filling #1), weave under and over like darning, making squares as shown.

Starting across broadest part of shape, with contrasting color, pick up the first threads diagonally at intersection slipping needle through from A to B as shown. (Do not sew through the material.)

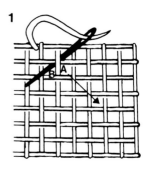

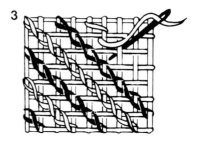

2 Work diagonally across as in diagram. Go through the material at C, and up at D, and start working upwards; take up threads at intersection exactly as when working downwards. Do not pull too tightly.

Now repeat #2 using another contrasting color, leaving one intersection clear between the lines of stitching. Cover the entire shape in this way, alternating lines of color and leaving one intersection clear between each line.

* SQUARED FILLING #3

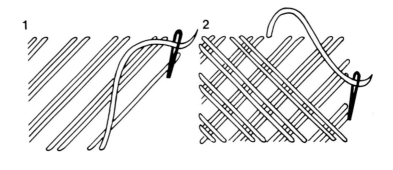

Lay parallel lines diagonally across the space to be filled, two lines close together though not touching, then a wider space, then two closer again, and so on (as shown).

Using the same color, repeat #1 in the opposite direction to make diamonds.

Using another color, fill each large diamond with Satin Stitch. To start the stitches evenly, put one stitch across the center, then two or three small stitches on either side.

With a third contrasting color, tie down the crisscross lines with four stitches coming up in the Satin Stitch and going down in the center, thus forming a star. When you tie down with these four stitches, be certain to maintain the space between the diagonal lines so a little material shows through (as shown).

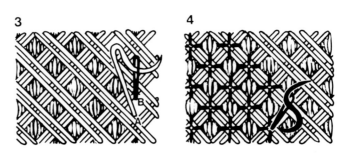

Squared Filling #3 may be shaded by changing the color of the Satin Stitches in the diamond.

* SQUARED FILLINGS #4/#5

#4. Both patterns have a base of squares tied down at the corners as in Squared Filling #8. For Filling #4 work four Detached Chain Stitches converging at one point, as shown. Place them in checkerboard fashion, leaving four empty squares between each block. Then work four French Knots close together in the corners of the empty squares, using a contrasting color.

#5. Work exactly the same way as #4 but leave a clear line of squares around the blocks of Detached Chain Stitches. Then work five Slanting Satin Stitches in the blank square connecting the corners of the blocks, as shown.

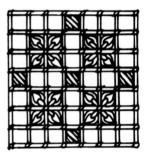

* SQUARED FILLINGS #6/#7

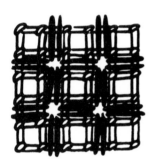

#6 and 7. First lay a foundation of squares and tie them down as in Squared Filling #8. For #6, work two stitches side by side (not touching) right over the squares, radiating them from a central square, as shown.

For #7, work a cross right over every other square, checkerboard fashion, but do not allow the crosses to touch one another.

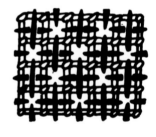

* SQUARED FILLING #8

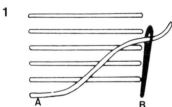

Coming up on one side of shape, make a long stitch right across, going down on other side. Fill the whole shape with exact parallel lines about ¼″ apart.

Then lay threads in the opposite direction, making perfect squares.

Tie down these squares at the corners with small stitches, all slanting in the same direction, as shown.

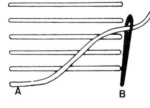

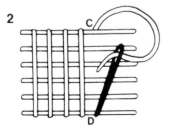

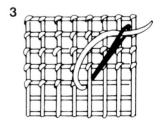

Using a contrasting color diagonally crisscross the whole design with long lines, first in one direction across the center of every other square, then in the other direction, so that the threads cross exactly where the basic square threads crossed. In this way a series of stars is formed, each with eight bars radiating from the center.

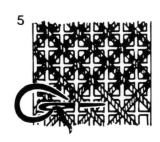

Using a blunt needle and with another contrasting color, tie down these diagonal lines where they cross and converge with the basic squares. To do this, come up on the left of one of the "square" lines and weave round in a circle, passing over the diagonal and picking up the "square" lines as you go round. Go down through the material just on the right of where you came up. Do not pull the circle too tight or it will disappear. A strong contrast in color is needed to make it show up well.

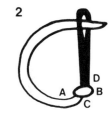

✶ SEEDING

Come up at A, and go down at B a small distance away. Pull through, lightly.

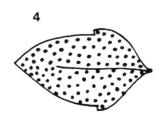

Come up at C and go down at D, across the first stitch, diagonally. Pull through, so that the stitch forms a firm, round, slightly raised "bump" on the fabric.

The finished effect appears as one raised stitch instead of two. When worked with thread which matches the background fabric in color seeding gives an attractive textured effect.

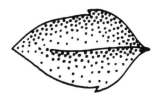

Stitches scattered evenly, each slanting in a different direction.

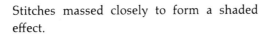

Stitches massed closely to form a shaded effect.

STEM STITCH

Needle comes up at A, goes in at B, and up again at C, exactly half way between A and B. Draw through, holding the thread to the left of the needle.

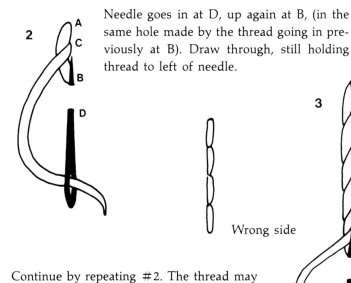

Needle goes in at D, up again at B, (in the same hole made by the thread going in previously at B). Draw through, still holding thread to left of needle.

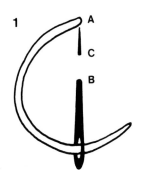

Continue by repeating #2. The thread may be held either to the right or the left of the needle, but should remain on the same side once the work is started.

Wrong side

∗ PADDED SATIN STITCH

The top row of Padded Satin Stitch may be worked straight instead of slanting, but this is much harder to make even, especially when the stitches are small at the point of a leaf. It is therefore best to practice it on a slant first.

Starting in the center of the shape, come up at A, down at B.

Fill shape with stitches just side by side.

Go across with a few stitches to hold the long ones flat.

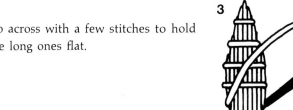

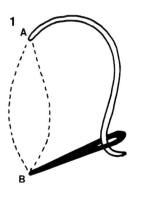

For the second padding, go up and down vertically again as in #2.

Come up at A, down at B, and cover the whole shape with slanting stitches as shown. To maintain the slant, A should always be a fraction ahead of the last stitch, and B should be pushed up very close to the previous stitches. (Otherwise the slant becomes flatter and flatter until it is almost straight.)

✳ RAISED STEM STITCH

Though it is shown here as a banding stitch, Raised Stem may be used to fill whole areas. In this case the long basic stitches should be tacked down invisibly here and there, afterwards. The stitch may be shaded, working in vertical bands, or stripes of contrasting colors. When used to fill an uneven area it usually needs an outline of Stem Stitch.

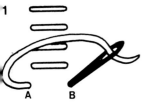

First work a series of parallel stitches (just under ¼″ apart, as shown in diagram). *To work a wider area than the one shown, lay these lines across the whole width of the shape.*

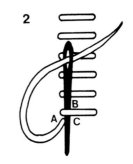

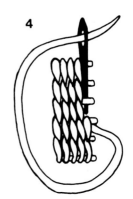

Using a blunt (tapestry) needle, come up at A, and holding thread to left of needle slide under first thread from B to C. Do not go through material.

Repeat #2, sliding needle under thread from D to E, and work up to top of thread in this way.

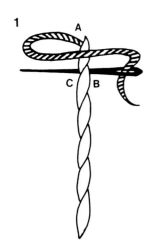

Work several lines close side by side always beginning again at the bottom, working upwards until base threads are entirely covered. Do not pack too many rows in, however, or the effect will be lost.

WHIPPED STEM STITCH

Whipped Stem Stitch makes a fine smooth line stitch when the Stem Stitch is whipped with the same color. (The Stem Stitches should not be too long.) An attractive candy cane effect is obtained if a contrasting color is used for the whipping. Generally it is best to use double thread in this case.

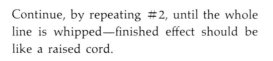

First work a line of Stem Stitch.

Then coming up at A change to a blunt tapestry needle and go through from B to C where stem stitches overlap one another. Pass only under the stitches, not through the material.

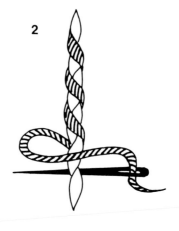

Continue, by repeating #2, until the whole line is whipped—finished effect should be like a raised cord.

CHAIN STITCH

Chain Stitch may be used as a solid filling, working row upon row closely side by side. Do not pack the stitches *too* closely, however, or the effect will be lost. The filling is equally effective if the lines are shaded, or worked all in one color with contrasting outline. (The stitches should all begin at the same end and run in the same direction to make a smooth effect.) When extra lines have to be added to broaden the shape in one place, add them on the inside, allowing a continuous line to run along the edges. In this way the joining lines will not be obvious, especially if the first stitch of the joining line is tucked *underneath* the longer line.

Chain Stitch may also be used as an outline where a fairly broad dominant edge is needed.

Bring needle up at A. **1**

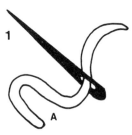

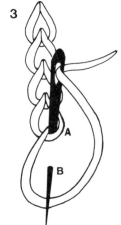

2

Form a loop, and put the needle in at A again, holding loop down with finger. Then come up at B, directly below A. Draw gently through, forming the first chain stitch.

3

Repeat #2, always inserting needle exactly where the thread came out, *inside* the last loop—come up directly below, and draw through so chain stitches lie flat on material. When filling a shape by working rows of Chain Stitch, always work in same direction, beginning each new row at top and working down.

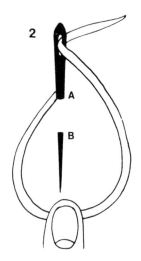

Wrong side

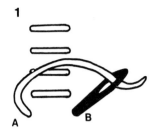

1

First work a series of parallel stitches (just under ¼" apart) as shown in diagram. (As for Raised Stem Stitch.)

* RAISED CHAIN STITCH

See notes on Raised Stem Stitch (page 47).

Then bring thread up at B and slide under thread from C to D (do not go through material). This stitch is best worked with a blunt needle. Draw through and hold thread upwards keeping it rather taut.

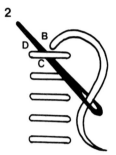

2

3

Next slide needle downwards under same thread, but to the right of first stitch, from E to F, draw through, holding thread under needle; do not pull too tightly so the appearance of the stitch is as in #4.

Continue stitch by repeating #2 and #3. Several rows may be worked side by side to fill a space (as in Raised Stem Stitch) instead of single row shown. In this case end off row at base and start again at the top, ready to work downwards.

4

WHIPPED CHAIN STITCH

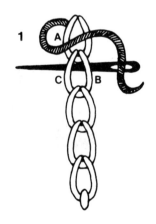

1

First work a row of chain stitch (see page 48). Then change to a blunt tapestry needle, come up at A, and slide needle through from B to C. Pick up the chain stitches only, do not go through the material.

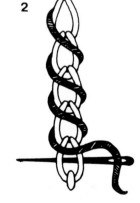

2

Continue, sliding the needle lightly under each chain, without pulling the thread too tightly. The finished effect should be like a raised cord.

BUTTONHOLE STITCH

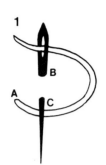

This is one of the most versatile of stitches. It may be worked in solid rows, or radiating from one central point to form a circle, in scallops, or with the spokes outwards as an outline around a shape. (This was frequently used in Jacobean embroidery to soften the edge of large leaves.) Always space the stitches just far enough apart to allow the loops at the edge to lie smoothly. Like Chain Stitch, Buttonhole Stitch is the basis for many other stitches, notably Coral Stitch.

Needle comes up at A, goes in at B, and up at C directly below B, and level with A. Thread is held under needle as in diagram. Draw through downwards.

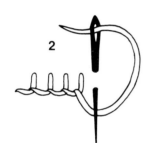

Next stitch repeats #1 at an even distance apart. Stitching may be spaced as shown, or worked closely as in #3.

Diagram shows angle of needle when working curved shapes.

*RAISED BUTTONHOLE

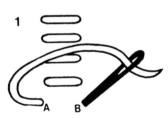

Using a blunt needle, come up at A, form a loop with the thread, and without going through the material, slide under the first bar from B to C (as shown). Draw down towards you until the thread is snug. This forms a Buttonhole Stitch on the horizontal bar.

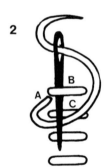

Repeat #2, sliding the needle under the thread from D to E, and work to the bottom of the bars in this way. When you have reached the bottom of each line, anchor the final stitch by going down through the material over the buttonhole loop at F (as in diagram #4).

Work several lines close side by side always beginning at the top, working downwards, until the bars are entirely covered. Do not pack too many rows in or the effect will be lost.

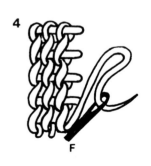

FRENCH KNOTS

French Knots may be scattered like seeding, to fill an area lightly, or they may be arranged in rows to fill a space solidly. The latter is most effective if each row is clearly defined and the knots lie evenly side by side. Alternatively they may be sprinkled closely but unevenly to produce an intentionally rough surface.

Bring needle up at A, twist thread once round needle as shown.

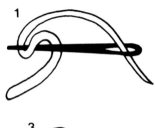

Put needle in at A, or just beside it, pull the thread until it fits *closely* round the needle (not too tightly). Pull needle through.

The finished knot. The thread should only be twisted once round the needle, as this makes a neat knot; *never* two or three times. The size of the knot is determined by the number of threads and size of the needle used.

BULLION KNOTS

Double thread is usually best for this stitch. The knots may be used individually, or worked side by side. They should not be too long, or they will curl instead of lying flat on the material.

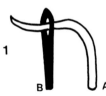

1. Bring needle up at A, go down at B, but do not pull thread through.

2. Stab needle up at A again but bring it only *halfway* through material.

3. Holding needle from below, twist thread round needle at A, until number of twists equals the distance between A and B.

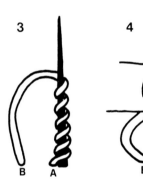

4. Holding top of needle and threads firmly with finger and thumb of left hand, draw needle through with right hand, loosening coil of threads with left hand as you do so, to allow needle to pass through freely.

5. Then place needle against end of twist, at the same time pulling on the thread, as shown, until the knot lies flat on the material. If any "bumps" appear in the knot, flatten these by stroking the underneath of twist with the needle, at the same time pulling on the thread.

6. Put needle in close, at the end of the twist and pull through firmly.

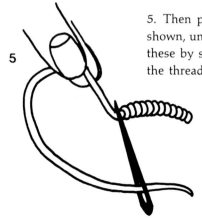

✳ SPIDER'S WEB/WHIPPED/WOVEN

Both Whipped and Woven Spider's Webs should be worked very tightly in the center to show the spokes clearly, loosening the threads slightly toward the outer edge. The spokes may be covered completely and the Spider's Web outlined, or just the center may be worked, leaving the spokes showing all round. One or several colors may be used for each web, and one or more threads, depending on the size.

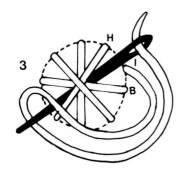

Using a blunt (tapestry) needle, come up at A, down at B, across center of circle.

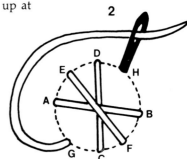

Then come up at C, and down at D (C to D should be slightly off center as shown). Come up at E, down at F, up at G and down at H. (H goes in quite close to D.)

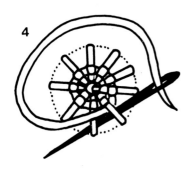

This leaves a space for the needle to come up finally at I, a point midway between H and B. Then slide the needle under all the threads at their intersection. Take the thread and loop it across the needle and then under it as shown. Draw through and pull upwards to knot threads together in center.

Whipped

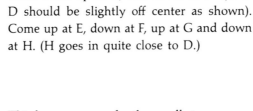

With the same thread, starting in the center, slide under 2 threads. Then place needle behind the thread just taken, slide under it, plus a new one. Progress in this way, back one and under two, till the spokes are all covered. Then either outline circle with Stem Stitch or leave plain.

Woven

Starting in center, weave under and over spokes, round and round, till whole circle is filled. Outline circle with Stem Stitch or leave plain.

* BRAID STITCH

Braid stitch is strictly an outline stitch, as it would be difficult to work rows close together without the needle interfering with the previous row. Single thread may be used, but double thread will show the stitch to its best advantage.

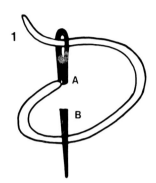

Make a small Chain Stitch. Come up at A, and go down again at A, holding the loop open—come up inside this loop at B and draw flat.

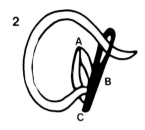

Anchor this Chain Stitch by going down outside the loop at C.

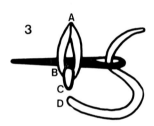

Using a blunt needle, come up at D and slide through the Chain Stitch (not through the material) from right to left (as shown).

Then go down at D through the material.

Next come up at E, just below D. Slide the needle from right to left under the anchoring stitch B-C, as well as the last chain just completed (diagram #4). Do not go through material.

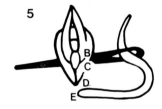

Go down through the material at E.

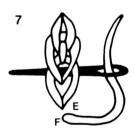

Come up at F and going back two stitches, slide the needle from right to left under both of them (as shown).

Continue in this way, sliding the needle from right to left under the two previous stitches together. Go down into the material where the thread came up, and come up again below ready to repeat.

The finished effect, drawn closely, is like a braid on top of the fabric.

* LAID WORK/TIED WITH CROSS BARS

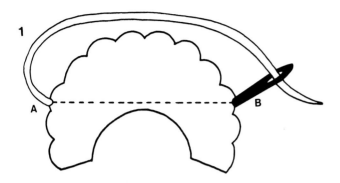

Laid Work may be used for large areas, since unlike satin stitch, no yarn is wasted on the reverse side. It may be held flat in many different ways by working other stitches on top in the opposite direction. Needle comes up at A, goes in at B right across widest point of shape, to establish desired direction. All subsequent stitches are parallel to this line.

Next stitch comes up at C close to B and goes down again at D close to A. When Laid Work is done correctly, very small stitches appear on the reverse side, while the right side is closely covered with long threads.

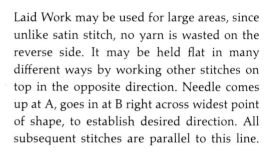

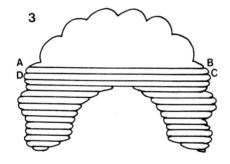

Continue working in this way, coming up close beneath previous stitch, on the same side as where you went down. (Stitches should lie evenly side by side with no material showing between them.) When lower half is completed go back to center and work upper half in same way.

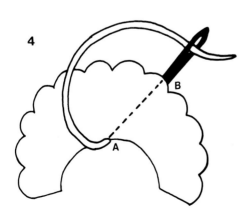

To hold Laid Work flat with Cross Bars, start in broadest part of shape and come up at A. Go down at B, laying a long thread diagonally across shape (angle is indicated by dotted line). This should cut across Laid Work threads at about 45°.

Hood, with a typically Elizabethan design, shaded with seeding and speckling stitches
Victoria and Albert Museum

* LAID WORK/TIED DIAGONALLY

First read basic Laid Work, 1, 2 and 3, page 54. Having worked Laid Work over area (in direction shown), come up at A, down at B. This stitch lies across broadest area of the shape, to set the correct angle for the following stitches.

Come up at C, down at D, making a line parallel to A and B, about ¼" above it. Then work from the center downwards until whole shape is laid with parallel slanting lines.

These lines must then be tied down with small stitches. Come up at A, down at B, going right through the material. These stitches should be placed alternately.

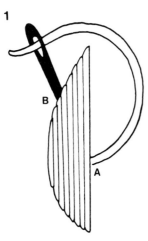

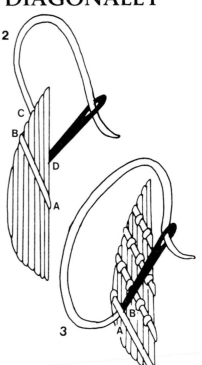

Black work techniques for a design adapted from a brass rubbing, worked in white on a black ground. *Designed and worked by the author*

WHITE WORK

*Arachne first invented working with the needle, which this mayd of Lydia learned from the spiders, taking her first samplers and patterns from them in imitation.**

—EDWARD TOPSEL, *History of Fourfooted Beasts and Serpents*, 1608

*Beautiful, young, and talented was Arachne—but boastful! She claimed she could spin and weave better than anyone in the world—even the goddess Athene. When Athene visited her, disguised as an old woman, Arachne unknowingly challenged her to a duel at tapestry weaving, which, of course, the goddess won. Arachne, in horror, hanged herself, and Athene, as a warning to all conceited mortals, quickly changed her into a spider so that she could spend eternity perfecting her stitches!

Close stem stitching on fine linen silhouettes the hunting figures. *Metropolitan Museum of Art*

WHEN Arachne first learned to imitate the spider, it must surely have been white work that became her first sampler! For nothing could be better compared with white work's textured patterns and airy openwork stitching than the lacy delicacy of a spider's web.

Because it is worked with white stitching on a white background fabric (hence the name!) white work needs a contrast of texture to give it its full effect. In fact, it is a sort of baccalaureate for the embroideress, an ultimate test of ability—for in its purity and restraint all depends on the excellence of delicate stitchery. Like a painter of still life, where the artist's true ability is shown without distraction of subject matter, the white-work embroideress has to channel her enthusiasm into the confines and limits of a monochromatic color scheme. A casual observer, accustomed to rainbow-hued crewel wools or exotic gold and silken threads, might be forgiven for not immediately appreciating its beauty.

Perhaps it needs an acquired taste, like that for caviar (to fit our idiom, the white Iranian kind, served only to the Czars!) to take delight in this form of stitchery which is not interchangeable with any other medium. Crewelwork may imitate oil painting, and silk embroidery, water color. Stump work may resemble sculpture, and needlepoint, tapestry. Even black work may be compared to etching. But white embroidery stands uniquely alone, its sparkling whiteness as refreshing as crisp air on a snowy winter's day. No wonder John Taylor, the seventeenth century's "Water Poet," referred to it in his book *The Needle's Excellency* as "frost work." "For Tent-Worke, Raised-Worke, Laid-Worke, Frost-Worke, Net-Worke—All these are good and this we must allow, that these are everywhere in practise now."

White work seems to have been done all through the ages in almost every country in the world. Sometimes it was in the ascendancy of fashion, sometimes overshadowed when other types of embroidery gained more attention. But it was always there—the delicate Indian muslins, the crisp white cuff that contrasted so beautifully with the Elizabethans' sparkling / 59 gold and silken sleeve; the Scandinavian openwork or the finely wrought Scottish baby bonnet—serving its purpose as a washable lightweight decorative cloth for shirts, underwear, bed pillows, coverlets, baby clothes, shawls, dresses, and altar linen.

The Egyptians were probably the first to use it, and it does seem logical that white embroidery would originate in countries where the finely woven background material was best suited to the tropical climate. Very primitive white work has been found in Coptic tombs; Cleopatra was known to have worn gossamer-drawn thread work; and when the Queen of Sheba visited King Solomon all his trumpet players were arrayed in white linen, which was more than likely to have been embroidered.

In China, it may have been closely related to the "forbidden stitch" (the French knot which was so fine and closely worked that the embroideress ultimately went blind!), for the finest work seems to have been done there since before recorded time.

Perhaps from China, Persia, Turkey, and Arabia, along the ancient trade routes, the tradition of the craft found its way to India where, on the banks of the Ganges and the Malabar Coast, a special caste of washer-*men* starched and pleated fine lightweight muslins for the Indian nobility. Princesses changed their clothes several times a day, a subject of amazement to later European visitors who seldom changed theirs at all!

The muslins were blanched with lemon water and given poetic Indian names such as "dew of light," "running water," "woven wind," and "scorched tears" and were so fine as to be almost transparent; in fact, a Dutch visitor to India in the seventeenth century wondered if the wearers weren't nude! These muslins were woven from the earliest days of India's history, for a historian describing the period from A.D. 320 to 420 wrote: "She wore a gown of white, bleached 'netra' cloth [a net with gold thread interwoven], lighter than a snake's slough, flowing down to her toes. Underneath gleamed a petticoat of saffron tint . . . a divine woman wearing a dazzling muslin robe embroidered with hundreds of diverse flowers and birds gently rippled by the motion of the breeze."

When the Portuguese navigators began to open India to the West at the turn of the sixteenth century, Vasco da Gama brought back, among the riches from the fabled East, a gift for the Queen of Portugal. It was a "white embroidered canopy for a bed, the most delicate piece of needle-work, like none other that has ever been seen; this has been made in Bengal, a country where they make wonderful things with the needle."

The tradition of needlework in India was certainly ancient, originally having been done to join and strengthen fabrics and eventually developing into a beautiful decoration.

One of the oldest literary documents in existence, the Rig-Veda, refers to it in a hymn in an invocation to Raka, the goddess of the full moon. "With never-breaking needle may she sew her work, and may she bestow on us a son who is worthy and will possess immense wealth." (The Hindu, by gifts and praise, always hoped to coax those invincible elements, such as the sun, the storm, and the lightning, into friendly acquiescence, and to provide him with the material things he needed.) This illuminates for us not only what an important part needlework played even in early Indian history, but also how valuable and fragile was a needle of hand-beaten gold, copper, or bronze.

The white embroidery that came from Madras, Delhi, Calcutta, and the area around the Ganges was called "Chikan." It was worked on filmy muslin which was woven from cotton, hemp, or the fiber of the pineapple

Detail from panel similar to the one on page 58

tree, and stiffened with rice starch. The embroidery was done with a double row of back stitches on the reverse side, which gave a shadowy effect. This was contrasted with an openwork stitch made by pulling a fine thread tightly to form regular holes in the gauzy fabric.

According to the Roman poet Lucan,* Cleopatra had robes which were made by a similar technique. In describing the fabric he said, "which wrought in close texture by the skill of the Chinese, the needle of the workman of the Nile has separated, and loosened the warp by stretching the web." Or, as he put it more romantically in verse,

> Her snowy breast shines through Sidonian threads,
> First by the comb of distant Seres struck
> Divided then by Egypt's skillful toil
> And with embroidery transparent made.

European embroideresses, accustomed to heavier linens, must have found the fine muslins fascinating, but the convolutions of the openwork stitch must have been almost impossible to unravel. For when the fine thread is pulled so tightly that only the open holes show, the method of working is completely concealed. Who knows, therefore, if a French or English lawyer might not have been inspired by that Indian name for muslin embroidery to add the word "chicanery" to the language to describe some particularly involved and intentionally deceiving piece of legal verbiage!

In Europe, where beautiful altar frontals were made in the thirteenth and fourteenth centuries in Switzerland, Saxony, and Germany, the white-on-white embroidery was worked with geometric patterns. Moorish tradition, which may have spread through Portugal, then at the height of its European influence, was perhaps the inspiration for filling the stylized designs with textural repeat patterns. These altar frontals were often done in convents. "Nuns with their needles wrote histories also," closely stitching and counting the threads of the fine linen to illustrate stories from the Scriptures for the unlettered. Many a wellborn lady who, jilted by her lover, had repaired to a nunnery, might have soothed her sorrows by sewing a design of the Annunciation of the Virgin, the Adoration of the Magi, or the Crucifixion of Christ. Similar embroideries were done in color, and

---

*Lucan was a young and romantic poet, who at the age of twenty-three was forced to take his own life, after an unsuccessful plot to overthrow Nero.

indeed these seem to be the forerunners of the later embroidery on canvas, but white to symbolize the purity of the Virgin was used for altar cloths and, for Lent, large hangings were worked as veils, hung to separate the altar and the choir from the congregation. Seen with soft light glimmering through them, silhouetting the shadowy figures with their rich variety of textured patterns, the designs must have appeared restrained and beautiful.

The linen was often woven in France and Germany, but the soil of Flanders and the Netherlands seemed particularly suitable for growing the flax. So excellent was the Dutch fabric that up until the eighteenth century, the word for the strongest linen was simply "Holland" or "Holland cloth."

Though fine, the linen was not transparent like the Eastern muslins, and sometimes the nuns would draw out the threads of the background to give a lighter effect. This led to a more openwork form of stitchery which they used for borders of sacramental and burial robes, keeping their methods a secret, and using the finest flax thread grown at Brabant and steeped in the waters near Haarlem. Besides, this openwork and drawn-thread embroidery was an ancient technique of knotting threads derived from fishnets. The *lacis* (network), as it was known in France, was then woven with solid patterns darned in and out with the needle. St. Paul's Cathedral in England had a cushion of this work in 1295 and Exeter Cathedral three pieces for "use at the altar."

Similar to *lacis* was hollie point, a needle lace made entirely of buttonhole stitch. The background of the pattern was solid, made by working the stitches close together, and the design itself was outlined by open holes formed by working the stitches wider apart. Was it called hollie point because of these holes, or because this early form of lace may have been of Arab origin and was brought from the Holy Land? No one is really sure.

Still another type of openwork, where buttonholed bars were connected across a linen surface which was afterward cut away, came from the Ionian Isles and Corfu, and was later known in Venice as Reticella. This "cut work," so called because the background was later removed, caused the astonishing and exciting discovery of the century—that a background linen was not really needed at all and that the stitches could be built up by themselves—and *"punto in aria,"* literally, "a stitch in the air," was born. This light and delicate stitchery became the first real needlemade lace, and Vinciolo, the Venetian who published a book of patterns for it in 1587 and who took it to France to the court of Catherine de Medici, became world famous. Venice, that glittering port, receiving the spoils of the fabled East brought back by Marco Polo, must have also received the finer, stronger, and more plentiful flax thread spun by the Saxon wheel invented in Nuremberg in 1530.

Not only was the sixteenth-century *punto in aria* new and different, it was available for the first time outside the church. For centuries thereafter all varieties of lace continued to be high fashion for costume and household articles, as well as church furnishings. Noblemen sold acres of land to be

Three examples of *punto in aria. Cooper Hewitt Museum of Design, Smithsonian Institution*

able to afford the expensive luxury. A French courtier of 1630 boasted that he wore "thirty-two acres of the best vineyard . . . around his neck." The plain sleeve edge disappeared for three hundred years, to be replaced by frothy layers of lace, and the collar, heavily starched, rose up to become a ruff, subsided to being a wide cape, and finally became a cravat, always made either entirely of lace or of fine linen bordered with deep bands and flounces of it. Knee breeches for men had wide frills of lace, and extravagant dress for both men and women was ornamented with gimps, braids, laces, and ribbons. The diarist Evelyn describes a fop at this time: "It was a fine silken thing I espied walking th' other day through Westminster Hall, that had as much ribbon about him as would have plundered six shops and set up twenty country peddlers. All his body was drest like a May-Pole, or a Tom o' Bedlam's cap. A fregat newly rigg'd kept not half such a clatter in a storme as this puppet's streamers did when the wind was in his shrouds; the motion was truly wonderful to behold."

Side by side with the needlemade lace or *punto in aria* in the sixteenth century, came the knotting of threads known as *macramé*, the forerunner, perhaps, of bobbin lace. Neither of these is really needlework, for true embroidery always must be worked on a background fabric, but both are so closely allied to it that they can really be considered as one. Thread knotting must have been at least as early a craft as embroidery itself; the necessity for knotting two threads together very soon developed into decorative bands and fringes. The trappings for horses, camels, and elephants shown in early paintings from the East clearly illustrate this. From earliest times, too, it must have been used by sailors, who on long sea voyages found it both amusing and practical. In fact, it was French sailors in the eighteenth century who gave it the name of *macramé*, and it was in that century that it really became the rage all over the Continent. Even Queen Mary of England, wife of William of Orange, was known as the Royal Knotter, "Who, when she rides in coach abroad,/Is always knotting threads."

It was said that "the Queen was oftener seen with a skein of thread about her neck than attending to affairs of state" and, "so fashionable was [this] labour of a sudden grown that not only assembly rooms and visiting rooms, but the streets, roads, nay the very playhouses were witnesses of this pretty industry."

In Queen Anne's time in England, the fashion for finely embroidered aprons worn by ladies as a purely decorative garment rose to a new height. Though many were done in silk and gold thread, white ones were popular, too. This fashion was decried by Beau Nash who, at a gathering in the assembly rooms at Bath, tore off the white apron worn by the Duchess of Queensbury and flung it into a corner, saying white aprons were worn only by serving women. With the advent of the neoclassic period and the interest in Greece and Rome came a fashion for white work dresses in muslin and gauze in devastatingly simple designs compared with what had gone before. Perhaps the fashion was a close reproduction of ancient marble statuary, for ladies clad all in white-on-white embroidery would go to balls in dresses dampened to accentuate their clinging filmy transparency.

With the development of Arkwright's and Crompton's looms, which meant that fine muslins and cottons no longer had to be imported from India, Britain began an industry of white embroidery which was highly successful until the late nineteenth century. Worked on a ring hoop or tambour frame (which gave the embroidery its name), it was done in chain stitch, sometimes with a fine crochet hook, like the Indian embroideries, and sometimes with a needle. Another type of white work, known as Broderie Anglaise, was done by cutting eyelet holes into the linen, which were then closely stitched around the edges. This, combined with tambour embroidery, was developed into a very competitive cottage industry in Ayrshire and Belfast. Cottagers would gather for the companionship of working together, pay a child a penny to keep the needles threaded, and contribute to the family earnings, though the highest pay was ten shillings a week for their labors.

In the eighteenth century a religious group from Germany settled in Bethlehem, Pennsylvania. They were the Moravian sisters, and they opened a school where they taught "fine needlework as an extra" for seventeen shillings and sixpence, Pennsylvania currency. Among the types of work they taught were tambour work, together with ribbon work, crepe work, flower embroidery, and pictures on satin. It is said that they embroidered Count Casimir Pulaski's banner, which his legion carried all through the Revolutionary War until his death at the siege of Savannah in 1779.

Perhaps the sisters fostered, or at any rate encouraged, the vogue for the "French embroidery" which became so popular between 1750 and 1840. Being similar to the Ayrshire work of this period in England, this embroidery was stitched by American ladies who made christening robes, baby bonnets, ruffled men's shirts, and gowns with long trains. At first the designs were done simply with padded satin stitch, but eventually all kinds of cut and pierced work gave way to real laces.

In the sixteenth century an English parson named Lee invented a knitting machine, but he died, disappointed and brokenhearted, without finding recognition for his work. Even Joseph Jacquard, who had just produced a net-making machine, when brought before Napoleon I, was asked, "Are you the man who pretends to do that which the Almighty cannot do, to tie a knot in a stretched string?" But the first patent for a machine which exactly duplicated hand embroidery on a multiple scale was taken out in 1829, remarkably enough, fifteen years before the machine for plain sewing was invented in America. The Jacquard loom, which was originally designed to reproduce knitting, was found to adapt magnificently to laces, and so in the nineteenth century modern science overtook the vast hand industry for white embroidery and lacemaking which had developed throughout the world.

Now that versatile and prolific machines can turn out as many thousand yards of white work as the trade demands, white embroidery by hand is done only in limited quantities by skilled professionals in places such as Hong Kong, Madeira, and Venice. This beautiful traditional work often passes unnoticed, most people imagining that such delicate stitchery could not possibly be done by hand.

Today, with the great revival of interest in handwork, the techniques of other centuries may be adapted to contemporary styles; if so, the results will be exciting and fascinating.

TO BEGIN

The most beautiful white-on-white embroidery can be worked with fine threads and delicate stitchery, to make such things as a monogrammed man's shirt, a throw pillow for a bed, a lampshade, table mats, a child's first dress, or an heirloom christening robe. The stitches can be as fairy-like and lacy as time and eyesight will allow, and the designs contemporary, even though you are using traditional techniques. But you can also take those techniques and expand them with dramatic results. Imagine a gauzy Dacron or organdy window curtain, shadow-stitched with snow-white angora on the reverse side. The bold wool stitchery (instead of the usual fine cotton) gives a clear opaque silhouette which contrasts beautifully with the sheer background fabric. Or visualize a Roman shade window curtain in coarse off-white linen with bands of needle weaving in natural rug wool. A wall hanging done with this large-scale openwork stitching could be illuminated from the back to show its airiness, or hung as a room divider to be seen from both sides.

One of the fascinations of white work is that instead of doing surface stitchery you really take a plain piece of fabric and transform it, either by drawing threads or cutting holes, or combining these with geometric patterns in self color to give a surface texture as well. There are literally hundreds of traditional variations on this theme, which go all the way from close solid stitching to needlemade lace. So many different styles and names may be confusing. Wherever do you start when confronted with names such as Hardanger and Hedebo, Richelieu and Reticella, Battenberg and Broderie Anglaise? But it is simpler than it seems, for basically there are only two main types of white work—coarse and fine. Coarse white, in spite of its name, may be worked on any *opaque* fabric which shows clear individual threads, from coarse burlap weaves to the finest linen. Then you count the mesh to make geometric surface textures, draw out threads to form lacy patterns and borders, or cut the material to make openwork holes.

Fine white is the type of stitching which is done when the linen is too sheer to draw threads, so the effect is made either by letting in net, working shadow stitch on the reverse side, or by drawing the fine threads

Example of Norwegian Hardanger embroidery. Geometric satin stitch patterns are worked on even-weave, double thread linen. Open work fillings are then cut as on page 76, and this drawn threadwork mesh is strengthened with needleweaving, page 79. Because the special double thread Hardanger linen is so firm, it can be cut close against the satin stitch without fraying. *Norwegian-American Museum*

tightly together to give an effect of open holes. This pulled stitching, as it is called, may also be done on coarse linen with a loose sleazy weave, so that large holes can easily be made in it. In other words, an open lacy effect is formed by pulling the threads together instead of drawing them out or cutting them.

So you can see that, opaque or transparent, it is the background fabric which really controls what type of stitching you do. If you start by making two samplers, one of coarse white and one of fine, you will be able to learn the basic techniques, recognize them when you see them in traditional white embroidery, and experiment with them and combine them in all sorts of different ways on future pieces of needlework.

COARSE WHITE WORK

MATERIALS, THREADS, AND NEEDLES

Use opaque linen of coarse, medium, or fine weave. Naturally, the fibers must be distinct enough to see the mesh clearly, and tightly twisted enough so that the threads can be drawn out without disintegrating. Monk's cloth, homespun, nylon or Dacron, and coarse wool or cotton as well as linen fabric may all be suitable. The best and sometimes the only way to tell whether a fabric is suitable is to take home a small swatch of it and experiment.

The traditional thread for coarse white embroidery is either tightly twisted linen thread or cotton embroidery floss—the six-stranded variety available in all notion stores. But, as suggested earlier, you could use any thickness of wool on heavy linen or any kind of white crochet cotton in various thicknesses.

Your needles must necessarily fit the thickness of thread you are using. They should be heavy enough to make a clear opening in the fabric

TOP, LEFT TO RIGHT. Monk's cloth; coarse open-weave linen; open-weave jute
BOTTOM, LEFT TO RIGHT. Natural coarse-weave wool; natural medium-weave linen; white medium-weave linen

so that the thread can follow smoothly, but if they are too coarse it will be hard to keep the stitching even. A package of assorted sizes embroidery, crewel, or chenille needles will be best, so that you can find exactly the right size for a particular stitch. For needleweaving you will need blunt tapestry needles since you are weaving between the threads of the background fabric, being careful to avoid splitting them.

TRANSFERRING THE DESIGN

Transfer your design by making a perforation, using carbon paper or tracing paper as shown on page 19. For the perforating method (page 20), use a very fine paintbrush and blue watercolor, since white work must be washable, and the blue paint will eventually wash out and will act like an old fashioned "blue bag" which will make the work appear whiter.

To position a design that may come in the four corners of a cloth or a table mat, fold the cloth in half diagonally and then in half again, creasing a diagonal line through all four corners (be certain not to stretch the fabric). Baste these diagonal lines across the cloth in both directions, using a contrasting thread. Place the design in the correct position in one corner, transfer it, and repeat in the other three corners.

THE STITCHES

TEXTURED SURFACE STITCHES

Flat geometric stitches
Padded satin
Seeding
Mountmellick stitch
Trailing

OPENWORK STITCHES

Drawn thread work borders
   with Hemstitching
Needleweaving
Open fillings
Cut work

Coarse white work consists of two contrasting types of stitches, those that are raised, giving textured interest to the surface of the material, and those that are open. In the first group are the geometric border and filling stitches, padded satin stitch, trailing, seeding, and Mountmellick stitch, to list some of the most basic ones. In the openwork group are drawn-thread-work borders, openwork fillings, and cut work.

*FLAT GEOMETRIC STITCHES

Using a blunt tapestry needle and an even weave linen so that the threads may be counted, you can work out geometric borders or fillings for silhouette shapes. These may be done in white on a colored linen, or in an entirely monochromatic color scheme such as white on white, or in a deeper shade such as natural on an off-white background.

You should use embroidery floss or heavy cotton to give you a crisp regular silhouette. Wool, with its hairy texture, is only suitable if a rough homespun look is desired.

White geometric stitches on a dark blue ground. *Author's Collection*

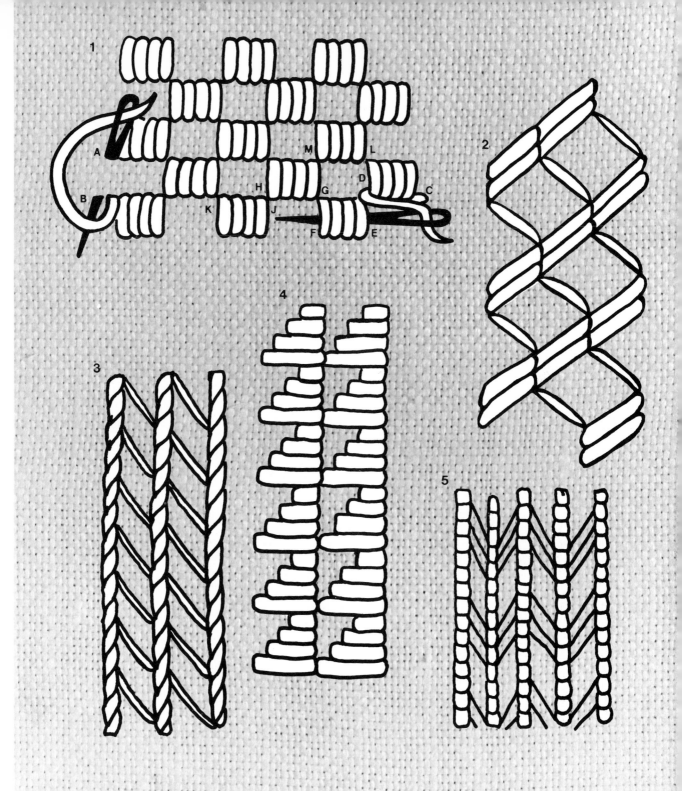

1. Make a chequer board pattern of blocks of stitches four threads deep, and four stitches wide, coming up at A, and going down at B. Then, using a blunt needle, weave through these blocks of stitches. Slide under the first block from C to D. Then go under the lower block from E to F. Slide through the next upper block from G to H, then go down and slide through from J to K and so on. The needle only slips under the stitches, not through the material. Repeat this on the next row above, starting through the upper part of block CD, then going through the next block above from L to M and so on. The weaving draws the blocks of stitches together making an even, slightly raised pattern. 2. Slanting stitches making a three-dimensional pattern. 3. Lines of stem stitch, connected by diagonal lines. 4. Blocks of satin stitch, counted out on the linen. 5. Back stitch combined with fishbone stitch in blocks of three

PADDED SATIN AND SEEDING

Padded satin stitch worked with fine cotton has a raised, shiny, very white effect which contrasts beautifully with openwork stitches in both coarse and fine white embroidery (see page 46).

Seeding produces a shadowy light effect which blends into the background and gives the material a textured appearance (see page 45).

Besides seeding and padded satin stitches, there are other surface stitches such as bullion knots, coral, chain, and whipped stem—in fact, almost the entire vocabulary of crewel embroidery, which can be very effective if used in white-on-white stitchery.

Bedspread showing raised white stitches. *Cooper Hewitt Museum of Design, Smithsonian Institution*

MOUNTMELLICK STITCH

Mountmellick is a surface stitch which has been used traditionally in white work only. It gets its name from the town in Ireland where it originated in the 1830's. It is a bold stitch with a raised effect, achieved by working heavy white cotton on a background such as satin or linen.

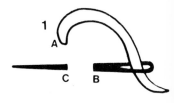

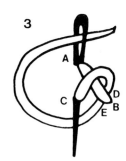

This stitch is worked vertically, and each individual stitch has three movements. Come up at A. Go down at B slightly to the right and below A, and come up at C directly underneath A. Pull through to form a slanting stitch.

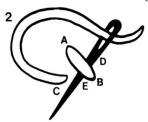

Slide under this stitch from D to E (do not go through the material).

Take a vertical stitch, going into the same holes from A to C, and looping the thread under the needle, draw through. This completes one stitch.

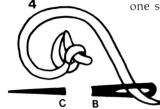

Repeat #1 again, taking another stitch under the first which is exactly like B to C at #1. Then repeat #2, sliding the needle under the slanting stitch as before.

Now repeat #3, but go down at the arrow right *inside* the previous stitch, just like a chain. Loop the thread under the needle as before, and repeat, to make a continuous line of stitches.

The finished effect. This stitch is best worked in heavy thread.

Corner of a cloth with Mountmellick stitch predominating. *Atlanta Historical Society*

*TRAILING STITCH with OPEN FILLINGS

Trailing is the most basic and useful stitch for white-on-white embroidery and is used in both coarse and fine white work. It is done by taking fine whipping stitches closely over a bundle of three or more loose threads, to form the effect of a smooth raised cord. Trailing may be used independently for linear designs; it may be used as an edging around other stitches, and when worked in double lines it makes a firm framework for openwork filling stitches.

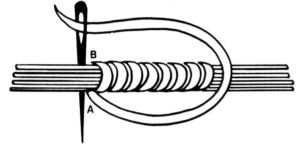 

Trailing

Come up at A, go over the bundle of threads and down at B, almost in the same hole as A. Repeat, placing each stitch very close side by side.

Trailing is done most easily with the fabric stretched tightly in a frame. As you take each stitch, pull the bundle of couching threads firmly in the direction you are working. This helps to make the line smooth and firm, like a cord (right above).

Open fillings (see opposite)

Working on clearly woven even-weave linen, outline the shape with two lines of trailing, side by side, worked one after the other. Then cut and draw out the threads of the linen inside the shape. Cut two threads and leave two threads in both directions, just inside the trailing, to give an over-all lattice effect as in the enlargement at left.

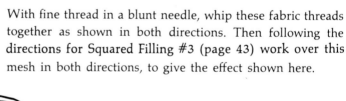

With fine thread in a blunt needle, whip these fabric threads together as shown in both directions. Then following the directions for Squared Filling #3 (page 43) work over this mesh in both directions, to give the effect shown here.

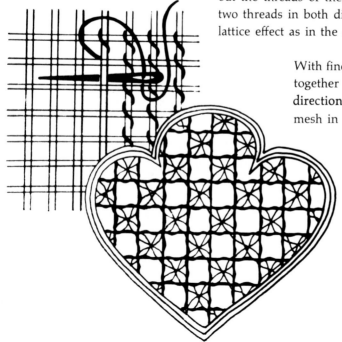

Openwork fillings are done by first completely outlining the shapes with two lines of trailing worked side by side. Then the linen is cut away close against the trailing, inside the shape, leaving alternate groups of threads uncut to form a trellis pattern. See sleeves and skirt, page 57. These threads are then whipped together to form a mesh into which other patterns can be woven, if desired.

Ornamental initial illustrating trailing, used as a pole screen, showing Mrs. Cabot's house in Murray Bay, Canada. *Worked by Mrs. F. Higginson Cabot and designed by the author*

DRAWN THREAD BORDERS

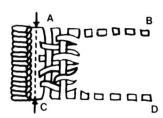

Determine the width and the length of the border you want to make, and draw one thread out of the linen on either side of it (at AB & CD). Then work a band of buttonhole (see page 50) between A and C, with loops facing inwards towards the border. Then work a second band at the other end. Next cut a vertical line between A & B (at arrows), carefully cutting each *horizontal* thread (*not* the upright, vertical ones). Repeat this at the other end, cutting close against the buttonhole stitching. Draw out the threads, one by one, until the border is composed only of vertical threads as at #2.

HEMSTITCHING

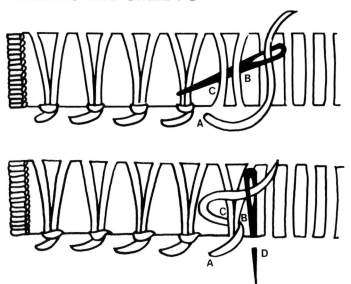

Secure the vertical threads of the border by hemstitching. Using a blunt, tapestry needle, come up at A, just underneath the border. Slide the needle under a bundle of two or more threads (from B to C).

Wrap round these threads and slide the needle into the fabric again at D as shown. Continue, repeating 2 and 3. Pull tight, and then hemstitch the opposite side of the border. Either hemstitch the same groups of threads to form a ladder effect, or split the groups, taking one bundle from one group and one from another, hemstitching them together on the opposite side.

NEEDLEWEAVING

Hemstitching the edges of the border is optional for needleweaving, it may just be left plain.
Prepare the border as in #1. Then, working on the reverse side, and using a blunt tapestry needle, weave over a bundle of approximately eight threads, then *under* a bundle of eight. The needle always goes down in the center of the two groups, first pointing from right to left, as shown, and then from left to right. Push the stitches together with the needle as you go, so that they are even and firmly packed. To end off, run the thread back under the stitching. Needleweaving may be done over three or even four groups of threads, or woven with many variations, some of which are shown on the opposite page. Each block of needleweaving shown here has been alternated by a single bundle of threads closely wrapped round and round.

Sampler of drawn thread borders. *Designed and worked by the author*

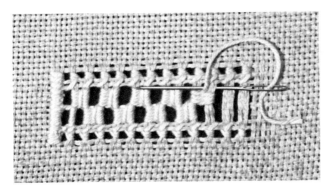

Needleweaving; in crochet cotton, above, and in coarse wool, right

BRODERIE ANGLAISE

The shapes to be cut are first strengthened by outlining them with running stitch around the edges. The fabric is then cut inside these shapes, leaving hems which are turned back and closely oversewn right over the running stitches. If the holes are so open that they might gape, they are held firm by working bars across the wider parts. Instead of simple oversewing (traditionally used in Broderie Anglaise and Danish Hedebo), sometimes buttonhole stitch is used instead. Richelieu is the name usually given to this type of work. The buttonhole bars of Richelieu may be further ornamented with small "picots," or decorative loops, which give the plain edges a frosty appearance (see page 93).

Round eyelets:

With a long enough thread to complete the working of a circle, make a line of running stitches all around the outline.

Leaving the thread hanging, cut four slits in the material from the center, out to the running stitch, as in the diagram.

Fold back these four flaps, one at a time, and closely sew over and over all around the edge, working right over the running stitches.

In the finished effect the oversewing stitches should make a smooth, narrow banding round the edge. Cut off the frayed turn backs on the wrong side. Small holes should not be cut, but pierced with the closed ends of a pointed pair of scissors or a stiletto, after outlining the eyelet with backstitch (below) instead of running.

BACKSTITCH

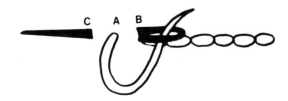

Come up at A, go down at B, then up ahead at C. Repeat, going back into same hole as the previous stitch. Keep all stitches the same size.

ABOVE. Dress with hand-worked panel of Broderie Anglaise. *Designed and worked by the author*
BELOW. Detail of a petticoat from a Roumanian peasant costume

FINE WHITE WORK

MATERIALS, THREADS, AND NEEDLES

Organdy, sheer Dacron, lawn, batiste, transparent loosely woven linen and wool, muslin, net—in fact any sheer fine white fabrics of varying opaqueness may be used for this embroidery.

Just as in coarse white, the most usual traditional thread for fine white is six-stranded embroidery floss, but there is no rule which says you may not use white angora, for instance, on organdy, for shadow work in bold scale. For pulled stitches, such as point Turc and point de Paris, the effect is made by holes. Therefore the thread should be fine and strong, and match the background fabric as closely as possible. Use a fine linen thread for this when you are working on an open weave linen, and a fine sewing silk or just one thread of six-stranded embroidery floss on lawn or organdy.

The needles you must use for punch stitch must be large enough to open holes in the fabric, so they should be quite heavy in comparison

TOP, LEFT TO RIGHT. Fine-weave casement cloth; medium-weave casement cloth; open mesh curtain fabric
BOTTOM, LEFT TO RIGHT. Dacron organdy; scrim; batiste

to the size of your thread and background material. As you are sewing through the same holes several times, a blunt needle is ideal to avoid splitting threads and to keep the openings clear. On organdy, a tapestry needle #18 is best for this stitch.

The same blunt tapestry needle is good for darning stitches on net, so that you can weave easily between the mesh. If you are going to do fine trailing on batiste or lawn you will need a hair-like needle, perhaps a #10 crewel, to use with a single strand of embroidery floss.

Since your needles will depend on the kind of background material and threads you are using, a package of assorted size crewel or embroidery needles will be the best thing to keep on hand. Because crewel needles have long eyes, they are easy to thread even when they are very fine.

TRANSFERRING THE DESIGN

Transferring the design for fine white embroidery is very simple. You first outline the pattern on white paper with India ink or a fine felt marking pen. When it is completely dry, lay the fabric on top, positioning it correctly, secure it with masking tape, and lightly trace the design onto the fabric with a very hard pencil (2H). Always be sure the paper with your design is *white*. If your design is on tracing or layout paper, put several other layers of paper underneath it. The more contrast between the white paper and the black design lines you have, the more clearly will your design show through the material. Never use too sharp a pencil for transferring the design since it may cut through the cloth.

If your fabric is too opaque to use this tracing method, you could use the tissue paper technique explained on page 20.'

If you are going to work on net you must transfer your design to oilcloth or similar vinyl or plastic material. (Plastic-coated shelf paper is good.) You can then baste your net to this and embroider the whole design, weaving and darning the stitches, following the outlines, which clearly show through the net. Your blunt needle will not penetrate the plastic because it glances off the shiny surface, and your work will not stretch out of shape because it is basted to this firm background. When you have completed your design, separate the plastic by removing the basting stitches. This same method is used for the openwork stitches of needlemade lace, known as point or Renaissance lace.

THE STITCHES

SURFACE STITCHES

Trailing
Seeding
Padded satin
Chain stitch
Shadow stitch
Shadow appliqué

OPEN STITCHES

Pulled stitches (point Turc
and point de Paris)
Darning on net
or tulle embroidery
Net inserts
Needlemade lace
(Renaissance or point lace)

SURFACE STITCHES

Trailing (page 76), seeding (page 45), and padded satin stitch (page 46) are excellent when used in combination with one another, and really look beautiful on both opaque and sheer fabrics. Seeding on transparent fabrics forms a shadow effect as the thread passes from one stitch to another on the back. The result is white close stitching instead of the light speckling, formed when seeding is worked on an opaque ground.

One of the great advantages of working on sheer fabric is that you can obtain shadow effects. Certain stitches give you a clear silhouette which stands out beautifully against the transparent background. Shadow stitch (a row of close herringbone stitches worked on the reverse side), is one of the best of these.

Shadow stitch is done by working close herringbone (also known as double back stitch) across the area of design, on the reverse side of the fabric. The stitches, crossing on the back, give a solid or lacy white effect, depending on how closely they are worked.

DOUBLE BACKSTITCH or SHADOW STITCH

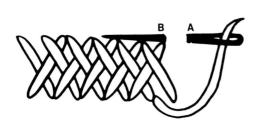

On the reverse side of the design, work a row of herringbone stitches. Take one stitch from right to left (A to B) on the lower outline of the design, and repeat it at the upper edge, going right into same hole formed by the previous stitch.

White shadow stitch combined with colored silk on organdy tablecloth. *Designed and worked by the author*

Reverse side

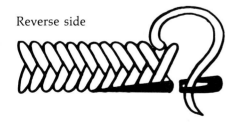

The effect is best if the stitches are taken very close together, as shown here.

When worked on sheer material, the effect on the right side is an opaque band bordered by a row of back stitches, above and below. The closer the stitches, the more opaque and distinct this band will be.

Right side

CHAIN STITCH AND SHADOW APPLIQUÉ

Chain stitch in white cotton provides a bold contrast when worked on a sheer background such as ninon, organdy, or filmy batiste. A similar effect can be obtained by stitching another layer of the same fabric either to the front or the back of the background material. This is known as shadow appliqué.

Shadow appliqué is done by basting another piece of the background cloth or another white material of contrasting texture such as satin to the *reverse* side of the transparent background. On the *right* side of the fabric, the design is then outlined with point Turc or point de Paris (pages 88, 87). Finally the extra material is cut away close to this stitching on the back.

The word shadow seems a misnomer for these techniques, for it is actually the surrounding fabric which appears to be shadowed, contrasting with the whiter effect of the design.

Shadow appliqué with point de Paris outlining the shapes. *Author's Collection*

OPEN STITCHES

Point Turc and point de Paris (Turkish stitch and pin, or Paris, stitch) can be done either on open weave linen or on any fine materials such as lawn, muslin, organdy, or silk.

The effect of both point Turc and point de Paris is a series of openwork holes made by pulling the fabric tightly together with fine thread. These holes then become dominant and the connecting stitches almost invisible (see page 89).

POINT DE PARIS

This stitch is particularly useful for holding 2 pieces of fabric together, so it is shown here used for a hem.

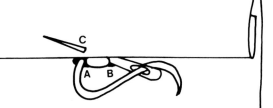

Using a blunt tapestry needle, come up at A under the hem, go in at B and return again at A in the same hole.

Go in again at B, and come up at C, directly above A in the hem.

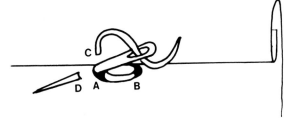

Return again to A, and come up at D.

Now repeat steps 1, 2 & 3, wrapping each stitch tightly to form large holes.

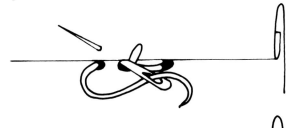

Shows finished effect.

PUNCH STITCH or POINT TURC

1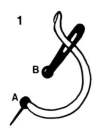

Using a blunt needle and fine thread come up at A, go in at B (above and to the right of A). Then return to A again. (The needle is slanting.)

2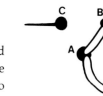

With the needle horizontal, go in at B again and come up in C, level with B (but beyond A). The distance from A, B, and C should be the same, so that they form a triangle.

3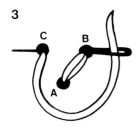

Repeat #2, going from B to C again, with the needle horizontal.

4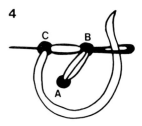

Take this BC once again, forming a double stitch. (Again the needle is horizontal.)

5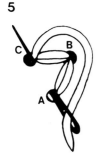

Go in at A and up at C. (The needle is slanting.)

Go in at A and up at D, level with A, but beyond C so that AB, BC, CA, and AD are all the same size stitches. (The needle is again horizontal.)

6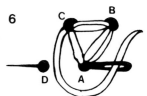

7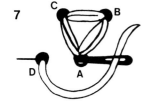

Repeat #6 going from A to D with the needle horizontal.

Repeat once more with a horizontal needle to make a double stitch from A to D.

8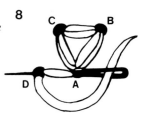

Repeat steps 1 to 8 to make a line of stitches. This diagram shows the way in which the stitch is worked.

9

#10 shows the finished effect. Once the stitch has been mastered as in #9, pull each stitch tightly to open large holes in the fabric. The stitches should be so tight they almost disappear, and the entire effect is formed by the holes between.

10

Point Turc may be worked in individual lines, or rows may be worked back and forth to fill an area. If one line is worked over a flat seam, the raw edges may be cut away so close to the stitching on either side that the seam appears only as a row of decorative openwork.

Point de Paris is most suitable for hems, and is particularly effective in shadow appliqué; it borders the applied shapes with a row of openwork holes.

In order to hold the holes firmly apart, each stitch must be wrapped twice. Therefore, it is best to first practice point Turc and point de Paris with heavier thread, working loosely, so that you can clearly see each stitch and master the repeated movements of the needle.

When you have learned how to do them, work with a single strand of embroidery floss and a large blunt needle and *pull tightly!* If you are working on lawn or organdy, use a tapestry needle #18, but once you have realized the effect you want to achieve you can find the needle which best suits the fabric you are using. Because you must pull tightly, work in your hand, wrapping the material firmly round your finger to hold it taut as you stitch. The lightness of the background fabric, the large size of the needle, the fineness of the working thread and the firm way you pull your stitches, all control the size of the holes.

Point Turc combined with chain stitch. *Designed and worked by author*

DARNING ON NET, TULLE EMBROIDERY

Mark out your design with a permanent felt-tipped pen on any stiff, shiny blue paper. A suggestion might be to use self-adhesive wallpaper (without removing the protective backing) or heavy duty plastic-coated shelf paper.

When the design is thoroughly dry, firmly baste your net to this paper and proceed to weave the outlines and patterns, following the lines which show clearly through the net. Use six-strand embroidery floss, varying the number of threads according to the effect you want, lacy or bold. Use a blunt needle which will slide easily over the plastic, and between the threads of the net without splitting them. Outline the shapes first with running stitch, using as many as six strands of cotton for a heavier effect. Then fill the shapes with geometric patterns, counting the threads of the mesh and using only one or two strands of cotton for a lacy effect.

Pattern #1

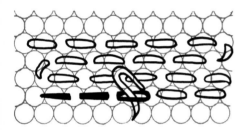

Care must be taken in starting and ending threads, as all joining will show clearly. End off if necessary by running a few threads back beside the ones you have just taken on the outlines. Preferably join by making a lace knot (page 95). This means you can join a new thread to your working one and continue stitching. The tiny knot will disappear invisibly into the embroidery.

Pattern #2

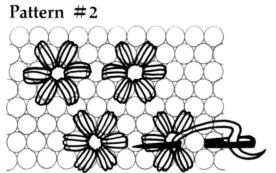

Pattern #3

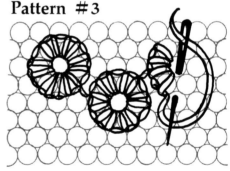

Pattern #4

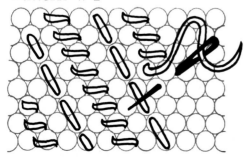

Pattern #5

Darning on net. A frame is useful for working the filling stitches. *Designed and worked by author*

NEEDLEMADE LACE

The variations of needlemade lace are too many to mention, but the simplest, point or Renaissance lace, is composed of braids which are knotted and looped together by buttonhole stitch.

Machine-made braids, which were available in the nineteenth century, but are now hard to get, may be replaced by making your own braids of hairpin lace or buying ribbons.

Start by outlining the design, with double lines, on blue plastic-coated paper, as on page 90. Then baste the braids or ribbons down within these lines, folding and tacking them where necessary. Then work buttonhole bars and spiders' webs to connect them, using a blunt needle, and embroidery floss or crochet cotton. Connecting stark white braids or ribbons with these bold simple stitches gives a dramatic effect, but alternatively all kinds of lace stitches, based on buttonhole stitch, can be worked to give a delicate or more solid effect, depending on the thickness of the thread.

Renaissance lace mats with braids held together by looped stitches and spiders' webs in coarse cotton thread. *Author's Collection*

NEEDLEMADE LACE/Spider's Web

Baste the ribbons, braids, or bands of hairpin lace to firm paper (such as vinyl, coated shelf paper), in any openwork pattern (see opposite).

Fold or pleat the braids if necessary to form smooth curves (at A, B, and C) and hem them together where they join each other (at arrow).

Then with a blunt needle and firm thread (such as buttonhole twist), connect the braids with bars. The circle shown here has threads crisscrossing the center (from D to E, F to G, etc.) so that a spider's web can be woven (see page 52, diagrams 3, 4, or 5). Conceal the threads by running through the braids as invisibly as possible from one bar to the other, and join on new threads with a lace knot (page 95) to save ending off.

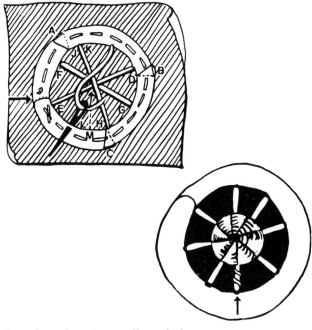

Shows the finished spider's web. To pass invisibly from one place to another in the openwork part of the design, wrap the working thread several times around one of the bars (at arrow).

When the whole design is finished, cut the basting threads to free the needlemade lace. (Cut them on the reverse side of your paper backing, to avoid cutting your stitches!)

NEEDLEMADE LACE with Buttonhole Bars and Picots

First baste the braids in position. Using a blunt needle, connect the braids with three bars, ending the final bar on the left, so that you can work close buttonhole stitching over the bars to the center. Slide the needle downwards into the last buttonhole stitch, and twist the working thread three (or more) times around it, as shown.

Draw through, holding the twists between finger and thumb, just like a bullion knot (see page 51). Then slide the needle upwards through the same buttonhole stitch, and pull through. Finish buttonholing the bar right across.

Shows the finished picot with the completed buttonholed bar. Buttonhole bars with picots may be used in cut work, as edgings, or with any open work or surface stitching as well as needlemade lace.

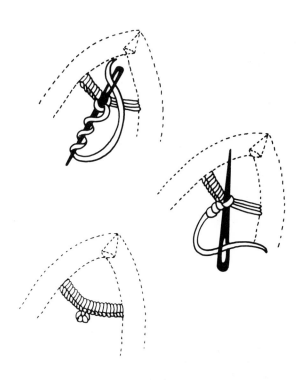

DETACHED BUTTONHOLE FILLING for Needlemade Lace

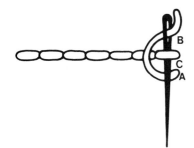

To work this stitch on fabric, first make a border of back stitch, as shown. For needlemade lace, take your stitches right into the braids themselves. This stitch is worked entirely free from the background. Using a blunt needle, come up at A on the right. Go through the first back stitch or braid from B to C. With the thread *under* the needle, just like a buttonhole stitch, draw gently through.

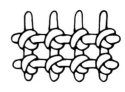

Repeat #1 to the left.

At left is the complete line, going down into the fabric or braid on the last stitch, to secure it.

At left is a second row, working again from right to left, and going into each stitch of the previous line, as shown.

For variation, a completely different effect can be formed when you work the first row from right to left, and the second from left to right, as shown here.

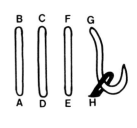

KNOTTED GROUND and DRAWN THREAD BORDER

First lay parallel threads across the area to be covered, coming up at A, down at B, up at C, etc.

Using a blunt tapestry needle, slide under the first bar from right to left. Take the working thread over, then under the needle and draw through, pulling gently upwards to form a knot.

Repeat on the next bar.

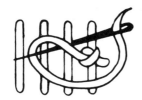

Shows 2 rows of knots worked over the ground threads.

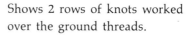

The same knot can be used to hold a bundle of threads together on a drawn thread border. Secure the thread in the center of the buttonholing at either side of the border.

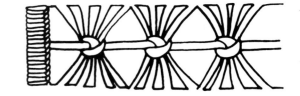

LACE KNOT

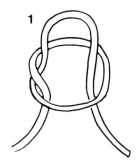

Begin as though you were making an ordinary knot in the thread, but instead of pulling the end through, pull through a loop as shown.

Push the end of the new thread to be joined through the top of this loop.

Holding the new thread firmly, pull the loop of the first thread tight.

When it is quite tight, pull sharply on *both* ends of the first thread. You will hear a little click as the new thread pops through the knot as shown here.

Pull both the first and the new thread tightly against one another to tighten the knot. The knot is so firm, if done correctly, that the ends may be trimmed quite short and the knot will be almost invisible. For needlemade lace and openwork filling stitches this knot enables you to work with a continuous thread, without ever having to end off.

FINISHING

Since white work is generally soft, pliable, or delicate it does not need blocking. Instead, it is best to soak it in cold water, and while it is still wet, press it face downward into a thick cloth. You can cover a Turkish towel or a blanket with a smooth hand towel or a sheet, and use this as a thick pad underneath.

LIST OF STITCHES